The Road to Heaven

Katheryn Maddox Haddad

Katheryn Maddox Haddad

Other Books by this Author

CHRISTIAN LIFE
Applied Christianity: Handbook 500 Good Works
You Can Be a Hero Alone
Worship Changes Since 1st Century
Worship 1sr Century Way
Inside the Hearts of Bible Women-Reader+Audio+Leader
The Lord's Supper: 52 Readings with Prayers

BIBLE TEXTS
Revelation: A Love Letter From God
The Holy Spirit: 592 Verses Examined
Was Jesus God? (Why Evil)
365 Life-Changing Scriptures Day by Date
Love Letters of Jesus & His Bride, Ecclesia (Song of Solomon)
Christianity or Islam? The Contrast
The Road to Heaven

FUN BOOKS
Bible Puzzles, Bible Song Book, Bible Numbers

TOUCHING GOD SERIES
365 Golden Bible Thoughts: God's Heart to Yours
365 Pearls of Wisdom: God's Soul to Yours
365 Silver-Winged Prayers: Your Spirit to God's

RESTORATION REPRINT LIBRARY
The Best of Alexander Campbell's Millennial Harbinger
Instrumental Music in the Public Worship of the Church
Church or Christ Writing 1600-1699, London

SURVEY SERIES: EASY BIBLE WORKBOOKS
→Old Testament & New Testament Surveys
→Questions You Have Asked-Part I & II

HISTORICAL RESEARCH BIBLE
for Novel, Screenwriter, Documentary & Thesis Writers

HISTORICAL NOVELS & STORYBOOKS
Series of 8: They Met Jesus
Ongoing Series of 8: Intrepid Men of God
Mysteries of the Empire with Klaudius & Hektor
Christmas: They Rocked the Cradle that Rocked the World
Series of 8: A Child's Life of Christ
Series of 10: A Child's Bible Heroes
Series of 8: A Child's Bible Kids
Series of 10: A Child's Bible Ladies

GENEALOGY: Climb Your Family Tree w/o Falling Out
Volume I & 2: Beginner-Intermediate & Colonial-Medieval

Copyright © 2018 Katheryn Maddox Haddad
NORTHERN LIGHTS PUBLISHING HOUSE

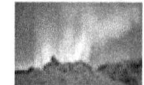

ISBN 9781952261152
Scripture taken from the NEW AMERICAN STANDARD BIBLE. Copyright @1960-1995 by The Lockman Foundation.
Used by permission.. Printed in the United States

ADJUSTMENTS FOR NON-CHRISTIAN READERS

I have published a variation of this book under the title WAS JESUS GOD?. That book was written primarily for non-Christian readers who have never read the Bible. At the beginning, it especially addresses issues Muslims have in what they are mistakenly told Christians believe.

All 546 scripture citations have been turned into endnotes to make reading smoother for them without the "interruptions". Also, in this way, they can look up the scripture citations if they choose to obtain a Bible and study the book after their initial reading.

WAS JESUS GOD? has more of an introduction for non-Christians. Further, neither one of the addendums in this book appear in theirs.

TABLE OF CONTENTS

1~JUST WHO IS GOD? 1
   God is One 1
   God, The Word 3
   What Did Jesus Call Himself? 5
2~GOD & THE PROBLEM OF EVIL 7
   Aristotle & God 8
   The Conscience 8
   What If The Laws Did Not Exist? 10
   Where did It Come From? 11
3~THE GHASTLY TRINITY: SATAN, SIN, DEATH 13
   Law of Nature 13
   Existence of God 13
   Existence of Evil 16
   Existence of Satan 17
   Definition of Sin 19
4-RANSOM 23
   The Capturing 23
   Two Kinds of Ransom 24
   Who are We Freed From? 27
   He Paid the Ransom to the Ghastly Trinity 28
   The Death Of Death 30
   Purpose Of The World 30
5~SPIRITUAL & PHYSICAL 33
   At War With Satan 35
   God Had To Become Flesh & Blood 35
   The Only Begotten 40
6~GOD Disarms Satan 41

A Part Of God	41
The Plan Is Carried Out	44
The Blood	45
7~JESUS' LIFE BEFORE HE WAS "BORN"	**49**
Jesus Always Existed	50
What Jesus Was	51
Whenever God Spoke or Appeared, That Was Jesus	52
8~GOD MATERIALIZED	**53**
Adam & Eve	53
Abraham	54
Abraham	54
Abraham	55
Hagar	55
Jacob	56
Moses	56
Balaam	57
Joshua	57
Joshua & Israelites	58
Gideon	58
Samson's Parents	58
Elijah	59
Shadrach, Meshach & Abednego	59
9~GOD APPEARED IN OBJECTS	**61**
A Whirlwind	61
A Stairway	61
A Burning Bush	61
Fire	62
A Pillar Of Cloud &/Or Fire	63
A Pillar Of Cloud	63
A Rock With Water	64

Jesus Was The Image Of The Invisible God 64
10~PROPHECIES OF JESUS FULFILLED 67
11~WHAT DOES JESUS DYING HAVE TO DO
WITH FORGIVENESS?.. 80
   What Things Are Sin?... 80
   Spiritual Laws That Cannot Be Broken...................... 82
   What Happens To Our Soul When We Sin?................ 83
12~WHAT IS SOUL DEATH? 84
   God Cannot Just Forgive Us....................................... 84
   God Had to Enter Our World..................................... 84
   God In Flesh Paid Our Ransom.................................. 85
   He Did What's Impossible For Us To Do.................... 86
   But Not Everyone Is Forgiven 86
13~WHY JESUS HAD TO DIE & COME BACK TO LIFE 88
   Adam: Physical & sinful... 88
   Mankind ~Physical & sinful Through Adam 89
   Abraham, Father Of Faith, Not Works 89
   Jesus, The Second Adam ~ Spiritual & Sinless 90
   He Bore Our Sins In His Body.................................... 92
   Mankind Spiritual & Sinless Through Jesus................ 93
14~WHAT ABOUT JESUS' THRONE NEXT TO GOD?... 95
   Not Two Thrones 95
   So, Where Is Jesus Sitting? 96
   What Is The Right Hand Of God?............................... 97
   Where Is He In Relation To The Throne Of God?......... 97
15~WHY ARE WE HERE?-I 99
   For God to Have Sons & Daughters 99
   To Rescue As Many As Possible 100
   To Strengthen The Heavenly Spirit World 101
   To Reveal The Mystery To 101
   The Spirit World... 101

To Explain Things To Angels	103
16 ~ WHY ARE WE HERE?-II	104
To Strengthen Us	104
Why Do We Need Strengthening?	109
17~HOW HARD IS IT?	111
We Don't Like Rules	112
We Think We're Good Enough	112
We Don't Get The Big Picture	114
Jesus' Apostles' Persecution & Death	121
Satan Just Thinks He's The Winner	123
18~JESUS' GLORIOUS BODY	125
His Body Had Healing Powers	125
His Body Could Walk On Water	126
His Body could glow like the sun	126
His Body Could Become Invisible	126
His Body Could Walk Through Walls	126
His Body Could Not Decay	127
His Body Could Change Shape	127
His Body Could Soar	128
His Body Seen Everywhere at Once	128
His Body is Recognizable to Everyone	128
And Our Body Over There?	129
19~SO WHAT ABOUT HEAVEN?	131
Terrible Things Happen in the Spirit World	132
Why War in the Spirit World?	134
We Are Part of that War	137
There is Only Room Enough in the Spirit World for God	138
God Never Promised We Would Be Everywhere	139
God will be With Us in the Heaven He Prepared for us	140
Addendum I	141

- A Few Additional Thoughts 141
- JUST WHO IS SATAN? 141
  - Is Satan's Name Lucifer? 141
  - Satan Falls Periodically 144
- ADDENDUM II 146
  - A Few More of My Thoughts 146
- DOES PARADISE STILL EXIST? 146
  - The Tree of Life 147
  - How Did the Tree of Life Get There? 147
  - Who are the captives? 148
  - When Can The Saved Go On To Heaven? 149

- Thank You 153
- ABOUT THE AUTHOR 154

- Buy Your Next Book Now 155
- Connect With The Author 156

- Get A Free Book 156
- Join My Dream Team 156

1~JUST WHO IS GOD?

We know there are only two elements in existence ~ mind and matter. Therefore, either matter made mind or mind made matter. If matter made mind, then nothing we think or imagine matters because matter in and of itself cannot think. If mind made matter, then there is reason and thought and the consequences of reason and thought do matter. As Dr. J.D. Bales, famous apologist of the Bible used to say with his quick wit, "If matter made mind, then it doesn't matter."

In Genesis 1:1-2 it says that God willed for heaven and earth to be created, God's Words spoke them into existence and God's Spirit (the life-giver) made it happen.

We know God is larger than the universe. How big is the universe? Scientists are now telling us our universe has over two trillion galaxies. Further, each galaxy has some one hundred thousand million stars. God is so large, he is impossible for the human eye to see. Further, the Bible says God is Spirit.

We do not have trouble connecting God the Will/Father and God the Spirit together. But we do have trouble connecting these two forms of life to words and a body. We know our body and words do not move and speak unless our will tells them where to go and what to say. We are not three; we are one. To help understand God as still being one, let us take a closer look at the oneness of God and it will open up a whole new world for you.

God is One

God is One, not many. When you speak into a audio recorder and your voice then comes out of that machine for other people to hear, that doesn't make you two. You are still one; you have just chosen to put your voice in something where you can be heard by more people or people far away. That audio recording is just another form of your voice.

You can stand in front of a movie camera and move around and speak. Then what you did can be shown on computer, television, and movie screens throughout the world. Does that mean there are now two of you ~ one in your body and one in the film? Or would that make hundreds of you ~ one in your body and one in each of the computers, televisions and theaters in the world?

God is One, and yet he revealed a part of himself in a burning bush to Moses just like you revealed a part of yourself in the audio recorder. Does that mean there were two Gods ~ one in heaven and one in the bush? No. God can reveal himself in different things if he wants to.

Today, God has his Word on paper and ink in a holy book. He has made his words visible to us in physical form. He is still not many Gods ~ one in heaven and thousands in his holy books around the world. He is still one God.

We need our body to show others what we are like. True, God doesn't need a body, but mankind, who dwells in the bodies he created for our minds to use, needed to see for themselves what God is like. So, God revealed himself in a body for a little while.

God can put his voice in a human being and that human say the exact words of God just like you can put your voice in a audio recorder and that recorder say the exact words of you. You can also put both your voice and body in a movie. God is still not two anymore than you become two.

God can put his words in a bush (as with Moses), in holy books (with paper and ink), and a human body (as with Jesus). God is still one.

God, The Word

Jesus is often called "the Word" or "God's Word". God watches people, but not with literal eyes the way we have them. In the same way, God can have a "son," but not in the literal sense that we do. John 1:1-3,14 in the Bible explains, "In the beginning was the Word, and THE WORD WAS WITH GOD and THE WORD WAS GOD....The Word BECAME FLESH and made his dwelling among us." Why? Because we needed to know how God would act with part of him in a human body.

Years ago during the black-and-white television era and early on the science fiction scene, there was a movie about a scientist who took the head of a woman just before her body died, kept the head alive, and set her on a table in his lab. Throughout the movie, she talked to the doctor. She was pretty and had a good mind, but none of that did her any good because she had no body to carry out the things she wanted to do. She was just verbal thoughts. She had a mind, she had a spirit keeping her alive, but no body. She could only think of things and speak of things, but she could never act on them.

That is God in the material world he made us. He has thoughts and plans and gave his words to the prophets to write down, but God himself, as long as he remained a spirit only, could not force humans to fully understand his thoughts and plans and how to live a good life with happiness.

You have an eternal mind/soul that is in your body right now. That body says and does things to show people what is in your mind/soul. But it is just temporary. When your body dies, you will live on because your body is not the real you. We are not a body with a mind/soul; we are a mind/soul with a body. Your mind, your eternal mind/soul, is the real you. In the same way, when God was in Jesus' body, that body was not God. The mind, the spirit, the heart and soul in that body was God.

We can be children of God. But it would be foolish to say Christians believe God had lots of wives and we became his children the way humans do. God "adopts" us and makes us his children. It is a spiritual thing, and wonderful.

Why would Jesus be called the only begotten Son of God, if he was not a son created in the literal way that we have sons? You have thoughts and those thoughts have existed as long as you have. But you still created those thoughts. When your thoughts become hearable or seeable, people call that your "brain child". In that same sense, Jesus was God's "brain child" ~ God's thoughts in hearable and seeable form. God was in Jesus in the same way that you are in a audio recorder or in a movie. You are still one and God is still one.

What about God saying he loves Jesus and is well pleased with him (Matthew 12:18 and 17:5)? Remember, Jesus was God's Words materialized in a body. We hear people say, "I hate my body." Or athletes say, "I'm proud of my body." People who lose weight often say, "I love my body." It was in this same spirit when the Father told the Son he loved him and was proud of him.

Conversely, some people who get depressed or experience mental illnesses say, "I hate my mind." As a result of a confused mind, they say and do things they regret. Remember, the Father is the mind, the will of God. Jesus is the Words and body of God materialized (John 1:1, Colossians 2:9, and Hebrews 10:5).

Jesus said in John 6:38, "For I have come down from heaven, not to do My own will, but the will of Him who sent Me." In John 14:31, he said, "I love the Father, I do exactly as the Father commanded Me."

So, what did God say and do in his materialized body we call Jesus? Acts 10:38 says Jesus went about doing good. What about his words? John 7:46 says "No one ever spoke the way this man does." After the Sermon on the Mount, the people "were astonished because he spoke with authority."

God materialized loved the things God the Will, the Mind determined for him to say and do. We humans do the same thing ~ we love or hate our bodies, we love or hate our minds but we are still one and God is still one.

What Did Jesus Call Himself?

Sixteen times in the Gospel of John Jesus referred to himself as "I AM". One or two times may not have meant anything, but he said it often. Compare this with what God called himself to Moses in Exodus 3:13-15 ~ the I AM.

I AM the bread of life come down from heaven (6:35 and 41)
I AM the light of the world (John 8:12)
I AM the Son of Man[kind] (John 8:28)
*Before Abraham was born, I AM (John 8:58)
I AM the door (John 10:7)
I AM the good shepherd (John 10:11 and 14)
*I AM the Son of God (John 10:36)
I AM the resurrection and the life (John 11:25)
I AM the way, and the truth, and the life (John 14:6)
I AM the true vine (John 15:1)

Jesus declared I AM three times at his betrayal (John 18:5 and 6 and 8)

I AM a king (John 18:37)

Jesus' enemies said he was making himself equal with God (John 5:17-18).

Jesus referred to himself when he quoted "And they shall be taught of God" (John 6:45).

Jesus said, "I and the Father are one" (John 10:30).

Jesus declared that he was in the Father and the Father was in him (John 10:38).

Jesus announced "He who sees Me sees the One who sent me" (John 12:45).

Jesus lamented, "If you knew Me you would know My Father also" (John 8:19).

Jesus explained, "He who has seen Me has seen the Father" (John 14:9).

Jesus said in his prayer, "You, Father, are in Me and I in You" (John 17:21).

Thomas told Jesus after his resurrection, "My Lord and my God!" (John 20:28) and Jesus blessed him for it.

Jesus called himself the Alpha and Omega ~ beginning and end, first and last (Revelation 1:8,17,18; 21:6,7; 22:13.) God said the same thing in Isaiah 44:6 and 48:12.

But, why did God materialize in our world?

2~GOD & THE PROBLEM OF EVIL

The road to heaven is complicated and only God understands it all. What we do know is that our road is from Satan to God. In order to understand Jesus ~ God in flesh ~ we need to understand evil, Satan, and death.

First, what is evil and how do we know it exists? We can only define evil by defining good. Most people, whether atheists or theists, would define good as a moral standard that does not hurt oneself or others. Those who are theists would define good further by saying it is the epitome of God, whereas evil is the epitome of Satan.

But many people today say there are different truths. "Your truth may be different from my truth." Everyone who has their own individual truth is still without excuse. The apostle Paul told the Gentiles who were without the Law of Moses and left to create their own understanding of God that they were still without excuse for their evil.

"That which is known about God is evident within them for God made it evident within them. For since the creation of the world His invisible attributes, His eternal power and divine nature have been clearly seen being understood through what has been made, so that they are without excuse" (Romans 1:19-20).

What did God make? He made (1) this material world and he made (2) mankind, the latter being in his image. Since God is a Spirit (John 4:24) his image is his attributes.

How did the Gentiles (most of the world) know God? "He was evident within them, for God made it evident within them."

Aristotle & God

"It is impossible for movement to come into being or cease to be, or that time should. There is Something which is capable of moving things or acting on them, but not actually doing so. It does not exercise what it causes.

"There are spatial movements ~ those of the planets ~ which are eternal, for a body which moves in a circle is eternal and unresting. The nature of stars is eternal and the Mover is eternal and prior to the moved.

"The First Cause is the cause of motion and eternal uniformity. There is something which is always moved with an unceasing motion in a circle. Therefore, the first heaven must be eternal. There is also Something which moves it without being moved, being eternal.

"Evidently there is but one heaven. The unmovable First Mover is one both in definition and in number. Evidently it thinks of that which is most divine and precious and does not change, for change would be for the worse.

"Life belongs to God, for actuality of thought is life. God's self-dependent actuality is life most good and eternal."

(Excerpts from Aristotle's *Metaphysics,* Book 12, chapters 6-8, 350 BC.)

The Conscience

Throughout the history of the world, mankind has had an inborn sense of right and wrong. True, in different parts or different eras of the world, the rules of right and wrong may be different. In one place, having three wives is considered right, but in another place, it is not. That is not what God put within us. Those are man-made laws.

Before God put within us any laws, he gave us a sense of ought.

Let us call it the inborn Law of Ought. If someone cuts in front of us in a line, we become angry and say, "You ought not have done that." If we catch someone lying to us, we say, "You ought not to have done that." If someone gossips about us or rams their car into our car or hits us, we say, "You ought not to have done that."

Or, if we see someone by the road who is suddenly injured, we tell ourselves, "I ought to stop and help that person." We may first consider any personal danger to ourselves if we stop to help the injured person and may decide not to stop, but deep inside we tell ourselves, "I ought to have stopped."

We add excuses to why we didn't stop, but still gnawing inside us is "I ought to have been braver than I am and stopped." This is a concept that helped former atheist, C. S. Lewis, work his way out of his atheism.

The conscience is explained in the Bible. The apostle Paul said conscience is an instinct. "For when Gentiles who do not have the Law [of Moses] do instinctively the things of the Law, these, not having the Law, are a law to themselves in that they show the work of the Law written in their hearts, their conscience bearing witness and their thoughts alternately accusing or else defending them" (Romans 2:14,15).

Paul said elsewhere, "But the goal of our instruction is love from a pure heart and a good conscience and a sincere faith" (I Timothy 1:5). On the other hand, he referred to "deceitful spirits and doctrines of demons by means of the hypocrisy of liars, seared in their own conscience as with a branding iron" (I Timothy 4:2).

"To the pure, all things are pure; but to those who are defiled and unbelieving, nothing is pure, but both their mind and their conscience are defiled. They profess to know God, but by their deeds they deny Him, being detestable and disobedient and worthless for any good deed" (Titus 1:15,16)

The writer of Hebrews said this in 13:18, "Pray for us, for we are sure that we have a good conscience, desiring to conduct ourselves honorable in all things."

What If The Laws Did Not Exist?

What about God revealing himself through what has been made? We have the Law of Nature that is consistently carried out without fail. If a rock comes loose on a mountain, it always falls. If too much water is in a glass or lake or stream, it flows over. At different times of year, the weather changes. During the day, the sun always shines. At night, it is always dark. The sun comes up in the east and goes down in the west. If you plant grass seeds, grass will grow. If you eat too much, you will become overweight. If you do not eat enough, you will become underweight. Consistency.

God does not say to the loose rock on the mountain, "I think I'll make you float up because you'll be more beautiful at the top of the mountain than trod underfoot at the bottom." He does not tell the sun to rise in the west because he is tired of the same thing all the time. There are no exceptions in the Laws of Nature. So, according to Romans 1:20, the things God has made reveal his inner nature too ~ consistency.

If there was no Law of Ought (conscience), we could tell tyrants what they are doing is okay because their law is just as important as anyone else's law. But we do not do that because of our sense of ought. A tyrant ought not to take people's land from them, he ought not to take their freedom from them, he ought not to take their homes from them.

Over and over through an average day, all humans struggle with this sense of ought. In our free time, we ought to have gone to see a sick person instead of mowing the lawn. In our free time, we ought to have spent time playing ball with an orphan boy instead of watching television.

Deep down, we know this. But we often do not give in to what we ought to be doing. When we answered the telephone, we ought not to have lied and said the person they asked for wasn't home when they really were home. Yes, even habitual liars know deep down they ought not to lie, but they think life would be better for them if they did. They have believed a lie about lying.

In war, each opposing side may be approached by a traitor and use their information to advance their cause, but each side despises traitors. Why? Because a person ought not to betray friends. A person ought to be loyal.

Where did It Come From?

Where did this Law of Ought come from?

There are only two elements in our existence ~ Mind and Matter. Which is stronger? Those who believe matter is all that matters believe matter just happened to appear for no particular reason, pieces of matter bumped into each other, a chain reaction occurred randomly through millions of years, and out of that came the stars, the planets, earth, things on earth and living creatures with different levels of mind and reasoning. Out of all that came life and mind. And those with the highest level of mind ~ humans ~ now have a sense of ought that objects and lower animals do not. All by accident.

Others believe Mind created all things with a design,

breathed life into them, and set in motion laws of nature and ought. What makes more sense? That Matter created mind, or Mind created matter? As Paul said in Romans 1, mankind can know God by the things he made ~ order, not chaos, not disorder, not randomness.

Solomon said there is a God-shaped emptiness in everyone's heart. "He has also set eternity in man's heart" (Ecclesiastes 3:11b).

The great Mind exists beyond our material world in a perfect world. We know by instinct that we cannot truly be happy unless we are in a society where everyone obeys that inner Law of Ought. But we know it is not happening in our world ~ in society in general as well as within our own selves specifically. Mankind has a longing that cannot be satisfied.

The apostle Paul explained it this way in Romans 7:14-24a.

"For we know that the Law [of Moses, but the same is true for the Law of Ought for Gentiles] is spiritual, but I am of flesh, sold into bondage to sin. For what I am doing, I do not understand; for I am not practicing what I would like to do, but I am doing the very thing I hate. But if I do the very thing I do not want to do, I agree with the Law, confessing that the Law is good. So now, no longer am I the one doing it, but sin which dwells in me. For I know that nothing good dwells in me, that is, in my flesh; for the willing is present in me, but the doing of the good is not. For the good that I want, I do not do, but I practice the very evil that I do not want. But if I am doing the very thing I do not want, I am no longer the one doing it, but sin which dwells in me. I find then, the principle that evil is present in me, but one who wants to do good. For I joyfully concur with the Law of God in the inner man, but I see a different law in the members of my body, waging war against the law of my mind and making me the prisoner of the law of sin which is in my members. Wretched man that I am."

3~THE GHASTLY TRINITY: SATAN, SIN, DEATH

Law of Nature

Take a long, hard look at the Law of Ought (conscience). It is a harsh law. It is unforgiving. The Law of Ought does not care how painful, dangerous or difficult something is. The Law of Ought tells us we should be willing to rush into danger to our own selves in order to help another. When we do not do it, something inside us makes us ashamed and we begin making excuses in order to ease our shame.

If we have decided that Mind made matter and set in motion the Law of Nature, then made humans and set in motion the Law of Ought, we compare ourselves to that Great Mind that always abides by its own laws. We feel like failures. We wonder if that Mind hates us. We wonder if we are enemies of that Mind which created perfection but which we continue to ruin.

Still, we have that longing, just as the apostle Paul did, to continue where we left off. Romans 7:24 says, "Wretched man that I am! Who will set me free from this body of Death?"

Existence of God

Mind or Matter?

The world we live in is made up of Mind and matter. Which came first? As quick-witted J. D. Bales, famous apologist of the mid-twentieth century, often said, "Mind made matter. If matter made Mind, nothing matters."

The cosmos is made up of hydrogen. Without hydrogen, no matter could exist. If matter is eternal and the cosmos is gradually using up its hydrogen, how could something that can be used up be eternal?

The cosmos is expanding. This means everything came from a single point. But matter wears out and grows smaller through time. Metal becomes rust. Water evaporates. Flesh turns to dust. How can something that wears out be eternal?

Before Time

If Mind made matter, Mind would have had to exist before matter and time since Mind created matter and time.

Genesis 1:1 says, "In the BEGINNING {time} God {First Cause} created {action} the heavens {filled with matter} and the earth {filled with matter}.

Whoever created time had to exist before time.

II Peter said in 3:8, "But do not forget this one thing, dear friends: With the Lord, a day is like a thousand years, and a thousand years are like a day."

Jesus, God in flesh, declared, "I am the Alpha [A] and the Omega [Z], the First and the Last, the Beginning and the End" (Revelation 22:13).

How do we explain eternity? Everything is now.

Before Matter

What can exist before matter and time? That which is eternal, beyond time and without a decaying body. John 4:24 says God is Spirit.

The prophet Jeremiah said, " 'Am I a God at hand, saith the Lord, and not a God afar off? Can any hide himself in secret places that I shall not see him?' saith the Lord. 'Do not I fill heaven and earth?' saith the Lord" (v. 23-24).

King Solomon said in II Chronicles 2:6, "But who is able to build a temple for him, since the heavens cannot contain him?"

David said in Psalm 139:7-12, "Where can I go from your Spirit? Where can I flee from your presence? If I go up to the heavens, you are there; if I make my bed in the depths, you are there. If I rise on the wings of the dawn, if I settle on the far side of the sea, even there your hand will guide me, your right hand will hold me fast. If I say, 'Surely the darkness will hide me and the light become night around me', even the darkness will not be dark to you; the night will shine like the day, for darkness is as light to you."

God is Logical

The apostle Paul said in his sermon on the Areopagus (Mars Hill) in Athens that God set in motion the Law of Nature so mankind would wonder how all this got here, "that they would seek God, if perhaps they might grope for Him and find Him…for we also are His children" (Acts 17:27, 29).

We know that nature ~ which we wish was perfect ~ goes awry with its hurricanes, earthquakes, floods, droughts, etc. as well as our longing for all people to be perfect.

Paul continues in Romans 8:19-22, "For the anxious longing of the creation waits [time] eagerly for the revealing of the sons of God. For the creation [matter] was subjected to futility, not willingly, but because of Him [God] who subjected it, in hope that the creation [matter] itself also will be set free from its slavery to corruption into the freedom [eternity] of the glory of the children of God. For we know that the whole creation [matter] groans and suffers the pains of childbirth together until now."

We have a longing to be perfect so we can be with the perfect God in his perfect world. We long for God to have personality because we long for God to love us during our time on this sometimes hostile earth. Is it possible when we feel so much shame for not always doing what we ought?

Many religions say God is just the essence of the universe without personality.

God proved he exists as a Person (not three persons) with personality. Remember, a person is an individual's character, the union of elements such as thoughts, body, emotions, sensations that constitute the individuality and identity of a person. How?

He proved it through his writings. The Bible is full of God's love for mankind, his disappointments, his reproofs, his corrections, his happiness, his sadness. The Bible is the only holy book in the world with built-in proofs ~ prophecies of entire kingdoms that were destroyed long after the prophecy was put into writing. If that is true, then the writings that reveal God's personality are true also.

Existence of Evil

If God made everything, he made evil. No, he did not.

Well, where did evil originate? Now we come to the Law of Parity.

God created light. But darkness exists. Darkness is the absence of light.

God created warmth from our sun. But cold exists. Cold is the absence of warmth.

God did not create goodness because he is goodness. Goodness is eternal. What is the absence of goodness? Evil.

There are numerous examples of the goodness of God in the Bible ~ love, holiness, unity, truth, harmony, health, peace, life, pleasure, faith, order, etc. What is the absence of these? Hatred, unholiness, disunity, fallacy, disharmony, sickness, war, Death, pain, fear, disorder.

Satan in Hebrew is *Abaddon*, meaning destroyer. Satan in Greek is *Apollyon*, meaning accuser. Satan accuses everything and everyone of being evil, then destroys them. He is an accuser, never a forgiver.

Existence of Satan

While we recognize the existence of a perfect God that always does everything that ought to be done and is therefore ultimate goodness and love, we must recognize the opposite exists: Evil.

Now we're getting to the cause of our dilemma, our failures, our not doing what we ought, thus putting shame in our heart and contributing to our imperfect world. Here are his attributes.

I John 3:8   Evil from the beginning

Revelation 9:11	Destroyer
John 8:44	A murderer from the beginning*
John 8:44	Father of liars
Job 1:6	Goes to heaven sometimes
Luke 10:18	Satan was falling from heaven as the 72 preached
Ephesians 2:2	Earth and air his empire
I Peter 5:8	
Romans 5:12-14	Through misrepresentation, he secured man's fall
Matthew 4:8,9	Lures people with force, greed, selfishness, ambition
John 12:31; 14:30; 16:11	Prince of this world
II Corinthians 4:4	God of this world
Ephesians 2:2	Prince of the power of the air
Matthew 7:22	Heads a host of demons
Hebrews 19:13	Has power of Death only on earth
Revelation 12:10	Accuser (unforgiver) of those God forgives
Job 1:6-11	Given power to test so good can prevail
Luke 31:32	Sifts believers
I Peter 5:8	Adversary, devours believers
Revelation 20:10	Will be cast into lake of fire forever
II Corinthians 6:15	Is the opposite of everything Christ teaches and stands for
Matthew 4:1	The devil
Matthew 13:39	The enemy
I Samuel 16:14	Evil spirit
I Kings 22:22	Lying spirit
Colossians 1:13	Power of darkness
Matthew 12:24	Prince of devils
Romans 16:20	Satan
Ephesians 2:2	Spirit of disobedience
Matthew 4:3	Tempter
Matthew 12:43	Unclean spirit
Matthew 13:19,38	Wicked one

Did you realize Satan is a father? He has children. Jesus said in John 8:44 he is the father of all liars. Do you ever tell a lie? I John 3:10 says anyone who does not actively practice righteousness is a child of the devil.

Satan has sinned from the beginning (I John 3:8) and has the power of Death (Hebrews 2:14).

So, to blithely pray to God, "Oh, and forgive us of our sins, Amen," is taking far too much for granted. Forgiveness is complicated, resulting in a complicated history of mankind.

Definition of Sin

Now, let us look at the definition of Sin based on the original languages the Bible was written in.

The basic Old Testament Hebrew word for Sin is *chet* or *chata* which means error or failure such as failure to make the goal of perfection. The other Hebrew word for Sin is *pesha* which means going over the border, to trespass, often translated transgress. In the New Testament Greek, Sin is *hemartia* which means error or failure, missing the mark.

Indeed, we humans continue to fail to live up to the Law of Ought. Instead, we trespass into the realm of Satan. In the list above, you see that Satan is a murderer and has been from the beginning.

God gave part of mankind the Law of Moses with 600 intricate laws to guide every part of their life. But no one could keep it perfectly and therefore be perfect. God let the rest of the world seek perfection their own way, but they could not be perfect either.

What is the ultimate result of our failure? Death. The Death of our souls. God warned Adam, "The day you Sin [eat from the tree of the knowledge of good and evil], you shall die" (Genesis 2:27).

It is obvious that Adam and Eve did not physically die the moment they ate the forbidden fruit. God said in Ezekiel 18:4b, "The soul that Sins shall die," but they did not die immediately. Adam and Eve went on to have sons and daughters. In fact, he lived another 800 years after having Seth.

Jesus said in Matthew 10:28, "Do not fear those who kill the body but are unable to kill the soul; but rather fear Him who is able to destroy both soul and body in hell." In Matthew 22:37, Jesus quoted the Old Law of Moses, "You shall love the Lord your God with all your heart, with all your soul, and with all your mind."

Thus, we see that our soul is the eternal part of us, while our body is the material, earthly part of us.

Now, let us return to Paul. In Romans 8:22-23 he says, "For we know that the whole creation groans and suffers the pains of childbirth together until now. And not only this, but also we ourselves, having the first fruits of the Spirit, even we ourselves groan within ourselves, waiting eagerly for our adoption as sons, the redemption [ransom] of our body."

Remember that yearning for us to do everything we ought to do in order to ease our consciences and take away our shame? Paul said in II Corinthians 5:1-4, "For we know that if the earthly tent which is our house is torn down, we have a building from God, a house not made with hands, eternal in the heavens. For indeed in this house we groan, longing to be clothed, inasmuch as we, having put it on, will not be found naked. For indeed while we are in this tent, we groan, being burdened, because we do not want to be unclothed but to be clothed."

What is holding us back? Satan, the devil. In the Old Testament, devil comes from the Hebrew word *shed*, meaning destroyer. In the New Testament Greek, devil comes from *diabosos*, meaning accuser.

And Sin personified pays wages to people who Sin. The reward, the wage of sinning is Death (Romans 3:23).

As long as we follow Satan, fall short of being perfect by sinning, our soul is dead and we are in Death's jurisdiction. Satan, Sin, and Death hold mankind for ransom, forever accusing and refusing to forgive.

Existence of Death

Death means separation. Physical Death is our separation from a presence on earth. Spiritual Death is our separation from God.

Death is often personified in the Bible. In the Old Testament, Job 28:22 declares "Abaddon [Satan] and Death say 'With our ears we have heard a report."

David said in Psalm 49:14 the evil people "are appointed for Sheol [grave]. Death shall be their shepherd."

Solomon advised his son in Proverbs 13:14; 14:27, "Turn aside from the snares of Death" instead fearing the Lord who is a fountain of life."

Isaiah warned that his people, the Jews, had "made a covenant with Death and with Sheol [grave]". He was speaking of what we today would call "selling our soul" for riches, power, beauty, etc. "Your covenant with Death will be cancelled." The prophet went on to say, "Sheol [grave] cannot thank you, Death cannot praise you."(Isaiah 28:15, 18; 38:18)

The prophet Habakkuk declared, "Death is never satisfied" (2:5). So true.

Death personified in the Old Testament is usually physical Death. In the New Testament, Death is usually personified as soul Death.

Over and over, the apostle Paul declared Death reigned

(Romans 5:12, 14, 17, 21). In Romans 6:9 he said Death is the master of those who Sin.

Sin and Death are often spoken of together: Romans 6:16 says Sin results in Death. Verse 23 says Sin pays the wages of Death to sinners.

James 1:15 says when someone Sins, he brings forth his own Death.

4-RANSOM

The Capturing

Satan wants to keep us in his domain, he wants to always control us. He is jealous of God and puts barriers in our way with his temptations through his followers which we continually give in to. Romans 3:23 says, "All have Sinned and fallen short of the glory of God."

Remember, "The day you Sin, you will die"? Remember, "The soul that Sins will die"? Remember, "Fear him who can kill the soul"?

First, being captured was our fault. Satan and his followers cannot force us to do anything. But they are masters at twisting the truth.

Satan would love to be god of the universe. But he has failed. So, he told the first humans, "Go ahead. Show your independence. Do what you're not supposed to, then you will be as smart as God ~ you will be equal to God" (Genesis 3:5). But God had warned, "Don't do it! You'll die."

Mankind stepped into the realm of Sin himself. Satan did not push us in. Satan set the trap and we walked into it. It is similar to wars where men wander too close to enemy lines, fall into their trap, then get captured.

"They may come to their senses and escape from the snare of the devil, having been held captive by him to do his will" (II Timothy 2:26).

Satan was a sinner from the beginning. Romans 5 says Adam took over from there. "Sin entered the world through one man, and Death through Sin, and in this way Death came to all people, because all Sinned.

As Jim McGuiggan explains in his audio series on Satan, Satan created the virus, he injected the virus into Adam, and the virus of Sin spread from man to man, generation to generation in an ever-growing pandemic.

The souls of every sinner were being held in Satan's realm and he intended for us to stay there. He never intended to let our Creator have us back. Remember, Satan is our accuser and destroyer. If he did not accuse and destroy, he could not exist.

Once captured, we became slaves to Sin (John 8:34; Romans 6). And remember, when we Sin we follow Satan and our wage is Death.

Two Kinds of Ransom

First of all, ransom is not the same thing as redeem or atone in the Bible. To redeem is to buy back what was God's in the first place. To atone is to purify and dissolve Sins with blood. The three are often used together, but are different and are different studies.

Second, there are two kinds of ransoms. Today we normally use the term "ransom demand." But that was not necessarily the meaning in Bible times. We find only four examples of ransom demands in the Bible and all are in the Old Testament using the Hebrew word *padah*.

PAID TO GOD WITH BLOOD for first born of every human and some animals (Exodus 13:13-15; 34:20, etc.)

PAID TO SLAVE TRADERS WITH MONEY by a man who

divorces a former slave (Exod. 21:8, etc.)

PAID TO VICTIM'S FAMILY WITH MONEY when an animal kills a human (Ex. 21:28-30, etc.)

PAID TO GOD WITH BLOOD BY man having sexual relations with engaged female slave (Lev. 19:20)

(We will discuss the significance of blood later.)

For the most part in the Old Testament, ransoms were paid to people who did not want to ever free their victims. The captor always considered the victims they had enslaved so valuable, no amount of anything would be enough to free them.

Victims asked God in prayer to ransom them, and it was always an almost impossible request. How does one get ransomed when the captor doesn't want the ransom? The ransoms were forced on them. Here is a list of ransoms forced onto the enemy:

FROM EGYPTIAN SLAVE OWNERS (Exodus. 6:6; 13:14).

FROM ATTACKING NATIONS (1 Chronicles 17:21)

FROM BABYLONIANS (USING PERSIANS) (Nehemiah 1:10)

FROM DEATH AND WAR (Job 5:20)

FROM ENEMIES (Job 6:23)

FROM ISRAEL'S TROUBLES (Psalm 25:22)

FROM DEATH (Psalm 49:15)

FROM BATTLE (Psalm 55:18)

FROM DAVID'S ENEMIES (Psalm 69:18)

FROM ENEMIES (Psalm 55:18)

FROM OPPRESSION OF MEN (Psalm 119:134)

FROM SIN (Psalm 130:8)

FROM WICKEDNESS (Jeremiah 15:21)

FROM STRONGER ENEMIES (Jeremiah 31:11)

FROM DEATH (Hosea 7:13; 13:14)

FROM SLAVE OWNERS IN EGYPT (Micah 6:4; 7:13, etc.)

The above scriptures are just representative because, in many cases, there are many scriptures saying the same thing.

The ransoms were not demanded by the captors. The ransoms were forced on them against their will with the boomerang method. So, keep in mind that most of the ransoms in the Bible were not money but by the will and power of God, the Omnipotent One.

Notice that most ransoms listed above were physical, but some were from Death, Sin, and wickedness.

In the New Testament, the Greek word *lutron* and variations is translated as ransom.

Further, with physical ransoms as examples of the earthly, ransom became spiritual in the New Testament. Ransom became soul ransom.

Titus 2:14 says we were *lutroned* FROM SIN (Titus 2:14).

Who are We Freed From?

It is popular today to say that we were ransomed from God's wrath or God's justice. That would mean God on the cross ransomed us from himself.

Not the Wrath of God

As Jim McGuiggan explains in his *The Dragon Slayer*, God became man, a representative of mankind, often calling himself the Son of Man. Look at Hebrews 2:11-15.

"Both the one who makes people holy and those who are made holy are of the same family. So Jesus is not ashamed to call them brothers and sisters. He says…

"For both He who sanctifies and those who are sanctified are all from one Father; for which reason He is not ashamed to call them brethren, saying, 'I will proclaim Your name to My brethren, in the midst of the congregation I will sing Your praise.' And again, 'I will put My trust in Him.' And again, 'Behold, I and the children whom God has given Me'."

"Therefore, since the children share in flesh and blood, He Himself likewise also partook of the same, that through Death He might render powerless him who had the power of Death, that is, the devil, and might free those who through fear of Death were subject to slavery all their lives."

Fleshly Jesus became part of the family of mankind. He was a son of Adam (Luke 3:23-38) who had introduced Sin into the world. He represented the family of mankind as explained in Romans 5 where he introduced sinlessness into the world as a representative of mankind.

"The entire family of mankind is subject to God's wrath so he can have mercy on us" (Romans 11:32).

The wrath of God is stern as any parent would be to save a rebellious child from ruining himself and being lost. God's wrath expresses his love, not his vindictiveness.

Never does the Bible say God's wrath was satisfied and obliterated on the cross. Just look at any concordance to see how often God's wrath is spoken of after Jesus died as an act of love.

Not The Justice of God

Nor is the justice of God satisfied. If that is what happened on the cross, why then do we still await another judgment?

God does not have a penal system for certain amounts and kinds of Sin. His sense of justice does not demand his "pound of flesh". Is God a divine legalist?

If God can only forgive us after the debt to his sense of justice has been paid, then what he gives is not true forgiveness. It's like sentencing a criminal, and after he has paid for his crime, saying we forgive the criminal. Is he a God who cannot forgive until the full penalty has been paid?

Would God be just to have Jesus pay the just penalty for our Sin on the cross, then have us pay the penalty for our Sin again on the Day of Judgment?

He Paid the Ransom to the Ghastly Trinity

As seen above, we are slaves to Satan, Sin, and Death ~ the ghastly trinity. If we are their slaves, then that is who are freed from.

When God forced ransom onto anyone, he paid them kind for kind. The way the Egyptians treated the slaves to force them to stay slaves is the way God treated the Egyptians to force them to free the slaves. The way the Babylonians treated the Israelites by destroying everything, including Jerusalem is the way God treated the Babylonians who were destroyed the same way by the Persians.

Satan wanted the Death of God and God wanted the destruction of Satan. Satan was the first sinner, he injected Adam with it, and it spread from there. The ghastly trinity ~ Satan, Sin, and Death ~ had to be dealt with.

The showdown took place during Jesus' ministry, came to a head on the cross, and culminated at the open grave.

Satan wanted God to hand his power over to Satan. That done, he could destroy God. Remember Jesus' temptation in the wilderness?

If Jesus had given in and turned the stones to bread, he would have been **obeying Satan**, exactly what Satan wanted. If Jesus had thrown himself down from the precipice of the temple, thus forcing the angels to rescue him, he would have been **turning his angels over to Satan**. If Jesus had bowed down to Satan, he would have been handing over **true life, love and truth to Satan.** Then there would have been no chance for mankind, no end to the pandemic of Sin Satan had created when he injected Adam with the virus and it spread unchecked from there through all generations.

The Death Of Death

Just what is Death? Basically, it means separation. For humans, it means separation from our spirit. You recall that, when someone dies, people often say (1) his spirit left his body. (2) It also means separation from life. (3) Death also mean separation from this world. Finally, since God is Life, (4) soul Death means separation from God.

The battle lines were drawn. What was God's goal? Revelation 20:10 says, "The devil who deceived them was thrown into the lake of fire and brimstone where the beast and the false prophet are also; and they will be tormented day and night forever and ever."

But that's not all. "The last enemy that will be abolished is Death" (I Corinthians 15:26).

Now we're beginning to see one of the purposes for which God created the world.

Purpose Of The World

Remember, this was all going on in the spirit world, but it affected us, and right here is the reason God created the world:

"To bring to light what is the administration of the MYSTERY which for ages has been hidden in God who created all things; so that the manifold wisdom of God might now be made known THROUGH THE CHURCH to the RULERS AND AUTHORITIES IN THE HEAVENLY PLACES [SPIRIT WORLD]. This was in accordance with the eternal purpose….For our struggle is not against flesh and blood, but against the rulers, against the powers, against the world forces of this darkness, against the spiritual forces of wickedness in the heavenly places [spirit world]" (Ephesians 3:9-11a; 6:12).

Jesus said that on the cross he would drive out the princ(ipality) of this world ~ Satan. See John 12:20-32 and 16:11.

Jesus came to disarm them and make them a spectacle ~ to embarrass them, to put them in their place before his angels and the world.

Erroneously, people declare, "I am saved" meaning they are saved to heaven. We are not saved to anything. We're saved from something. When we are drowning, we are not saved to the shore. We are saved from the water. So, when we are spiritually saved, we are not saved to heaven, we are saved from Satan, our captor. We need to always remember what we are saved from.

What was the mystery and who does not understand it? There are sixteen passages in the New Testament with the word "mystery". In every one, it points to forgiveness, being saved or ransomed. Saved from who? Satan. Saved from what? Hell. Why? Because we do not do what we ought as spelled out by God whom Satan hates.

These passages tell us that all humans understand forgiveness. So, who does not understand the "mystery" of forgiveness? "Principalities and powers in heavenly realms". In the next chapter is a chart listing these "mystery" passages, when the "mystery" began and when it is to be completed (fulfilled).

But for now, we need to concentrate on who the principalities and powers are who do not understand the "mystery" of forgiveness.

Romans 8:37-39 says "Death, angels, principalities, and powers" are among those who want to separate us from the love of God.

Ephesians 6:11,12 says the devil schemes through "rulers, powers, and world forces of darkness, spiritual forces of wickedness in heavenly [spiritual] places".

Colossians 2:10,12-15 says rulers and authorities battle against us.

Why did God have to prove anything to them? Good angels do not understand everything (I Corinthians 4:9; 6:3; Ephesians 3:10; I Peter 1:12). As Jimmy Allen, Bible professor at Harding University used to say, bad angels need to know why they are going to be doomed forever on the Day of Judgment (II Peter 2:4; Jude 1:6).

So sinful men stripped Jesus naked and held him up for public ridicule at the cross. At the same time, Jesus stripped these principalities naked and exposed them to the world so the world would ridicule them.

"When He had disarmed the rulers and authorities, He made a public display of them, having triumphed over them through Him" (Colossians 2:15).

And how is evil disarmed? Not with wrath. Not with justice. But with love.

5~SPIRITUAL & PHYSICAL

Forgiveness of our Sin is no simple thing. Over and over I hear prayers like, "Thank you for this new day. Guide, guard and direct us. Help your people the world over. Bless all those it is our duty to pray for, and forgive our sins. In Jesus name, Amen." And that's it. No second thoughts. We go merrily on our way.

We go through life blithely asking God, "and forgive us our sins" and think nothing of it. With the same blitheness, we say, "Thank you, Lord, for saving us." Saving us to heaven? That is not saving. We are saved from something. If we are snatched out of the way of an oncoming car, we are not saved to the sidewalk. We are saved from the car. Spiritually, we are saved from danger. We are saved from Satan and hell. Forgiveness is no simple thing.

Mankind was born with a sense of "ought" (conscience) that continually has plagued us because we could not be perfect and always obey that sense of "ought". God said the day we disobey, we will die. Satan is the King of Death and he kidnapped us after we crossed the line, put our souls in a state of Death, and held us forever ~ so he thought. It was battle time and God knew exactly what he had to do. But how? This was a battle in the spiritual world!

Remember, Satan is the ruler of demons (Matthew 9:34), the ruler of this world (John 12:31; John 16:11), the prince of the power of the air and of the spirit that is now working in the sons of disobedience (Ephesians 2:2).

Was Satan playing games at mankind's expense? Of course, he was. To him it was "Catching me if you can!" But it was no game to God. God knew when he created the earth and mankind what he was going to do.

God knew what Satan would try all along. Here is a chart listing the passages mentioning "mystery of forgiveness" and either when it originated or when it will be completed. [Blanks mean time is not mentioned.]

SCRIPTURE	TIME ORIGINATED	TIME COMPLETED
Matthew 13:10,11,34,35	From the foundation of the world	
Romans 10:1; 11:11,12,19, 25,27,35		When fullness of Jews and Gentiles completed
Romans 16:24-27	When the world began	
Romans 16:24-27	When the world began	
I Corinthians 1:2,17; 2:7,9		When the Lord comes
I Corinthians 15:50-57		At the last trumpet
Ephesians 1:1-4,9,10	Before the foundation of the world	Fullness of time when all gathered to Christ
Ephesians 3:3,4,9	From the beginning of the world	
Ephesians 5:30,32		
Colossians 1:23,26-28	Before all ages and generations	When Christians are presented to God
Colossians 1:1; 2:2,3		
Colossians 3:24; 3:3-6		When the inheritance is given
II Thessalonians 2:2-10		The day of Christ
I Timothy 3:15,16		
Revelation 10:6,7		At the seventh trumpet
Revelation 17:7-9,14,17	From the foundation of the world	When the Word of God is fulfilled

"Woe to the earth and the sea because the devil has come down to you, having great wrath, knowing that he has only a short time" (Revelation 12:12).

Yes, God knew this all along and his counterattack was always in place. Isaiah 35 unfolds it beautifully for us:

"Behold, your GOD will come with vengeance. The recompense of GOD will come, but he will save you. Then the eyes of the blind will be opened and the ears of the deaf will be unstopped. Then the lamb will leap like a deer and the tongue of the mute will shout for joy" (v. 4-6). Recognize anyone here? Who performed these miracles? Jesus did.

"A highway will be there, a roadway, and it will be called the Highway of Holiness....The redeemed will walk there" (v. 9b-10a).

At War With Satan

God fought Satan in heavenly realms.

"There was war in heaven. Michel and his angels waging war with the dragon. The dragon and his angels waged war and they were not strong enough, and there was no longer a place found or them in heaven. The great dragon was thrown down, the serpent of old who is called the devil and Satan, who deceives the whole world; he was thrown down to the earth, and his angels were thrown down with him" when Jesus died on the cross (Revelation 12:7-10).

Then God fought him on earth. "Now the ruler of this world will be cast out" (John 12:31b).

Later in this book we will discuss why God made us physical and put us on a physical earth instead of making us spirits and putting us in a spiritual world.

God Had To Become Flesh & Blood

God is a Spirit. Astronomers now estimate there are two trillion galaxies out there ~ not stars, but galaxies. And each galaxy has one hundred thousand million stars. We cannot begin to comprehend how large God is since he is more enormous than everything he created. He is so big, we cannot truly see him. It is like standing so close to a sky scraper we can see only one or two inches.

Further, since the Father is the will, this is another reason it is impossible to see God. You cannot see someone's will. You cannot see someone's mind. Our will and mind are part of our spirit, and it is impossible to see a spirit.

It is impossible for us to see God. Therefore, he cannot be completely understood. But he could be better understood and better of service to us if he had flesh and blood like us and we could see and hear him and tell future generations what we saw and heard.

God made our world material. He made us flesh and blood. Satan became the prince of this world, so God had to enter enemy territory where his children were. But God is a Spirit. Mankind is flesh and blood. God had to materialize.

I Timothy 3:15,16 refers to the, "...household of God which is the church of the living God....He who was REVEALED IN THE FLESH, vindicated in the Spirit, seen by angels, proclaimed among the nations, believed on in the world, taken up in glory."

"In the beginning was the Word, and the Word was with God and THE WORD WAS GOD....And the WORD BECAME FESH and dwelt among us" (John 1:1,14).

"He APPEARED in order to take away Sins." (I John 3:5).

Colossians 2:9 says Jesus was the full God in a body.

The book of Hebrews explains so many physical things as they relate to the spiritual. This is one of them:

"Sacrifice and offering You have not desired, but a BODY You have prepared for Me" (Hebrews 10:5).

"...the church of God which He PURCHASED [back from Satan, Sin, and Death] with His own BLOOD" (Acts 20:28).

"In Him we have REDEMPTION [were redeemed/ransomed/freed from Satan] through His BLOOD" (Ephesians 1:7)

"He RESCUED US from the DOMAIN OF DARKNESS" (Colossians 1:13).

Remember, arrangements were made for blood sacrifices the firstborns under the Law of Moses so they wouldn't have to serve God full time like the priests and Levites did? Numbers 18:17 said sheep and goats could not be redeemed/bought back by their owners. They had to die and their blood sprinkled on the altar. Now recall what John the Baptist said when he announced Jesus, "Behold! The Lamb of God who takes away the Sins of the world" (John 1:19).

Here are vital verses that explain God in the body of Jesus who came to pay the ransom for mankind to Satan, Sin, and Death. Remember Romans 6:26 that says, "The wages of Sin is Death." Jesus had to collect our wages, then he had to go one step further and, as God, die. Here are the prophecies of Isaiah again saying that God was our redeemer, that God paid the ransom by collecting the wages of Death.

41:14	...the Lord, and your Redeemer is the Holy One of Israel
43:14	...the Lord your Redeemer, the Holy One of Israel
44:6	...his Redeemer, the Lord of hosts
44:24	...the Lord, your Redeemer who formed you from the womb

47:4	Our Redeemer, the Lord of hosts is His name
48:17	...the Lord your Redeemer, the Holy One of Israel
49:7	...the Lord, the Redeemer of Israel and its Holy One
54:8	...the Lord your Redeemer
60:16	I, the Lord, am your Savior and your Redeemer
62:12	The holy people, The redeemed of the Lord.

Jesus paid the ransom and bought us out of slavery to Satan, Sin and Death and into freedom, and in the process redeemed us back to him, our original owner. How? By atoning (purifying) blood.

"...the weakness of your flesh. For just as you presented your members as slaves to impurity and to lawlessness resulting in further lawlessness....Therefore, what benefit were you then deriving from the things of which you are now ashamed? For the outcome of those things is Death. But now, having been FREED from Sin..." (Romans 6:18-21). "It is for FREEDOM that Christ set us free" (Galatians 4:31a). Acts 26:17-18 explains that Satan's power is darkness.

Paul explicitly speaks of, "Our great GOD AND SAVIOR, Christ Jesus, who gave Himself for us to redeem us..." (Titus 2:14).

"Then that lawless one will be revealed whom the Lord will slay with the breath of His mouth and bring to an end by the appearance of His coming; that is, the one whose coming is in accord with all power and signs and false wonders" (II Thessalonians 2:8).

Another apostle stated in II Peter 1:1b, "To those who have received a faith of the same kind as ours by the righteousness of our GOD AND SAVIOR Jesus Christ."

Paul referred to "...the church of GOD which He purchased (redeemed) with his OWN BLOOD" (Acts 20:28b).

Some people think we are redeemed TO heaven. Stop and

think. We are not being redeemed to something. We are being redeemed FROM something ~ Satan who wants to hold us captive. "...they may come to their senses and escape from the snare of the devil, having been held captive by him to do his will (II Timothy 2:26).

"In the beginning was the Word, and the word was with God and THE WORD WAS GOD....And the WORD BECAME FESH and dwelt among us" (John 1:1,14).

"His Son...through whom also He made the world. And He is the radiance of His [God'] glory and the EXACT REPRESENTATION of his nature" (Hebrews 1:3)

"....the glory of Christ who is the IMAGE OF GOD....the One who has shone in our hearts to give the Light of the knowledge of the glory of GOD IN THE FACE OF CHRIST (II Corinthians 4:4b-6).

"GOD WAS IN CHRIST reconciling the world to Himself....I WILL DWELL IN THEM AND WALK AMONG THEM; and I will be their God, and they shall be my people" (II Corinthians 5:19; 6:16).

"...by the righteousness of OUR GOD AND SAVIOR, JESUS CHRIST" (II Peter 1:2).

"Christ Jesus who, although HE EXISTED IN THE FORM OF GOD, did not regard equality with God a thing to be grasped, but emptied himself, taking the form of a bond-servant, and being made in the likeness of men, being found in APPEARANCE AS A MAN" (Philippians 2:6,7). He got that glory back that he had before the world began after his crucifixion and resurrection (John 17:5).

"The church of the living GOD...who was REVEALED IN THE FLESH" (I Timothy 3:15-16).

"But when the kindness of GOD OUR SAVIOR and his love for mankind APPEARED, He saved us."

"But of the SON He says, "Your throne, O GOD, is forever and ever" (Hebrews 1:8).

The Only Begotten

Jesus said he was the only begotten Son of God come to save the world from Satan (John 3:16). Begotten how?

"And the Word became flesh and dwelt among us and we saw His glory, glory as of the only begotten from the Father" (John 1:14)

Jesus was the Word of God. There was only one Word of God ~ the Bible. That made Jesus the ONLY.

"...God has sent His only begotten Son into the world so that we might live through Him" (I John 4:9)

What is the significance of being begotten of God? Isaiah explains it in 9:6.

"For a CHILD will be born to us, a SON will be given to us...and His name will be...Mighty GOD, eternal FATHER, Prince of Peace".

There it is! The child will be both Son and Father and be God. He was self-begotten, self-existent!

Micah 5:2 predicted the place of Jesus' birth thusly: "But as for you, Bethlehem...will go forth from Me to be ruler in Israel. His goings forth are from long ago. From the days of ETERNITY."

6~GOD Disarms Satan

Remember, God is a Spirit, but he put us in a material world. So, at times, it was not unusual for God to manifest himself on earth. It began in the Garden of Eden when he walked with Adam and Eve in the cool of the evening (Genesis 3:8). Surely Adam and Eve were not taking a stroll with a spirit.

Further, it was predicted, "…just as God said, 'I will dwell in them and walk among them; and I will be their God, and they shall be my people'" (Ezekiel 37:27 and II Corinthians 6:16). Of course, we know that was a prediction of Jesus.

Another chapter in this book tells of all the instances that God manifested himself to the world. The chapter is called *Jesus' Life Before He Was Born*.

So, Satan wanted to use his powers over Sin and Death to destroy God and his powers over good and life. The battle lines were drawn at the beginning, then the battle began. Whoever wins gets mankind for eternity. How do we know? Because that's what God did to free us. Many verses in the Bible speaks of Jesus freeing us.

A Part Of God

God decided to put a part of himself in human flesh. Which part?

Remember, humans were made in the image of God (Genesis 1:26). Notice Genesis 1:1,2 and John 1:1,2,14:

"In the beginning GOD" (the Great Determiner, the Will, the First Cause)…

"...created the heavens and the earth. The WORD SPOKE the world into existence and without the Word nothing was made.

"...And the SPIRIT of God was moving over the surface of the waters....and breathed into his nostrils the breath of life.

[As an aside, God did not create darkness. He created light (Genesis 1:3,4). I wonder if Satan was sparring with God even then.]

The Psalms tell of this event in a slightly different and more melodic way.

"Before the mountains were born or you gave birth to the earth and the world, even from everlasting to everlasting, You are God" (Psalm 90:2).

"By the WORD of the Lord the heavens were made" (Psalm 33:6a)...

"And by the BREATH [SPIRIT] of His mouth..." (Psalm 33:6b).

So, we see in these examples that there are three parts of God: (1) the Will, the Cause, the Determiner; (2) the Word that demonstrates and carries out the Will; (3) the Spirit that creates life.

We see here that God can materialize, and any time he does, that is His WORD (who we best know as Jesus).

So, to satisfy the ghastly trinity, God sent a part of himself ~ Jesus ~ to be in flesh awhile so Satan could convince God in flesh to Sin and send him to an eternal Death.

While the Word was in the flesh, he was 100% God the Word (John 1:14), but he was also 100% man, being born of a woman (Luke 1:26-32). Therefore, he had the same emotions and interests as a man. Hebrews 4:15 says Jesus was tempted in every way that all humans are tempted.

Jesus ended up voluntarily handing his life over to Death. It was not forced on him. It was not taken from him. He voluntarily gave it. "No one has taken it [my life] away from me, but I lay it down on My own initiative. I have authority to lay it down, and I have authority to take it up again" (John 10:18).

But the human side of him did not want to die on the cross. "In the days of his flesh, He offered up both prayers and supplications with loud crying and tears to the One able to save Him from Death" (Hebrews 5:7a).

Some people ask, "Well, if Jesus was God then whenever he prayed, was he praying to himself?". Closely associated with this is people saying, "If Jesus was God why did he say he could not do anything without his Father's permission?

"My food is to do the will of Him who sent Me and to accomplish His work....I can do nothing on My own initiative. As I hear, I judge; and My judgment is just because I do not seek My own will but the will of Him who sent me....For I have come down from heaven, not to do My own will, but the will of Him who sent me (John 4:34; 5:30; 6:38).

Each of us has three parts: (1) Our mind/will, (2) our words and actions, (3) our spirit. I Thessalonians 5:23 says we have soul, body and spirit. We say that, when someone dies, their spirit has left their body. Our words do not say anything and our body does not do anything without the determination, the instructions, the will of our mind. We don't just start talking without our mind telling us what to say. We don't just start walking without our mind telling us where to go.

In the same way that our words and actions have to obey our mind/will, Jesus the Word had to obey his Will.

Further, since the Father is the will, this is another reason it is impossible to see God. You cannot see someone's will. You cannot see someone's mind. Our will and mind are part of our spirit, and it is impossible to see a spirit. So, God's Words took on flesh.

The Plan Is Carried Out

Jesus died. Plain and simple. Jesus died. We have already looked at numerous verses that Jesus ransomed us, Jesus redeemed us, Jesus freed us from Satan, Sin, and Death with his blood and the Death of his flesh.

Satan was as terrified of God in flesh at the cross as he was at the beginning of Jesus' ministry and the great temptation. What did Satan say over and over? "If you are the Son of God, turn…." "If you are the Son of God, jump…" "If you are the Son of God, bow…." At the cross Satan through his emissaries said over and over, "If you are the Son of God." He tried to create doubt. He could not.

The first battle was won on the cross. Why? Because Satan and his followers were never able to make God in flesh Sin. Sin was Satan's partner. But stubborn Jesus died while still sinless.

Outcome: JESUS CONQUERED SIN FOR US.

Some people comment, "Well, if Jesus was God, then God was dead three days." Again, this comes from a physical mind, not a spiritual mind. That flesh was dead (though it did not decay) but not his Spirit.

The second battle was won at the tomb. Why? Because Satan's other great partner was Death. What did Jesus do with it? He grabbed Death up, shook it senseless, and trampled on it.

Outcome: JESUS CONQUERED DEATH FOR US.

Jesus was not really dead. That body was temporarily, but Jesus wasn't. He was in Paradise (Luke 23:43) alive and well.

Then, to rub salt into Satan's wound, Jesus returned to that body, walked the earth again for forty more days (Acts 1:3) and was even seen by five hundred people at once (I Corinthians 15:6).

Satan, Sin, and Death were now powerless. "Consequently, just as one Sin resulted in condemnation for all people, so also one righteous act resulted in justification and life for all people. For just as through the disobedience of the one man the many were made sinners, so also through the obedience of the one man the many will be made righteous" (Romans 5:18-19)"

Yes, Satan gave the virus of Sin to Adam and he spread the virus worldwide to all his descendants until we had a pandemic of sin that could not be stopped. Jesus came along with the antidote: Believe in him and he can make believers sinless vicariously through his sinlessness.

And Death? "Since the children have flesh and blood, he too shared in their humanity so that by his Death he might break the power of him who holds the power of Death—that is, the devil—and free those who all their lives were held in slavery by their fear of Death" (Hebrews 2:14-15).

The Blood

"You were redeemed with... precious blood as of a lamb

unblemished and spotless, the blood of Christ. For He was foreknown before the foundation of the world" (I Peter 1:19).

Why was blood so important? In the previous chapter we covered scriptures referring to God's blood. But what was the significance? Why did God insist people smear blood on their door posts so their first-born wouldn't die in Egypt (Exodus 12)? Why, for all those centuries, did God command the blood of goats and lambs be shed for people's Sin (Leviticus 48:27-35)?

Why, at the annual Passover week, were individual families to kill an unblemished lamb or goat, spread its blood on their door post, then eat the meat (Exodus 12:5-7)?

Why on the most important Day of Passover was the high priest to kill a bull and sprinkle part of its blood on the "Mercy Seat of God" over the Ark of the Covenant inside the Most Holy Place? Why did the high priest then kill a goat and sprinkle its blood in the same place? How did the blood bring atonement for the Sins of the people? (See Leviticus 11:1-16.)

Why did the high priest go to the altar in the courtyard and smear blood on the four corners of the altar where horns were placed? What did the blood have to do with atoning for the Sins of the people? (See Leviticus 11:17-19.)

And what were the people to do while the high priest was killing and sprinkling blood? "You shall humble your souls and not do any work... for it is on this day that atonement shall be made for you to **cleanse** you; you will be **clean** from all your Sins before the Lord" (Leviticus 11:29-30). Blood was a cleanser, a purifier.

What does atonement mean? Does it mean satisfying God's wrath or sense of justice? No. It means to reconcile. The high priest sprinkled the first of the blood on the "mercy seat" in the Holy of Holies, to indicate God's mercy. And on the horns of the altar to indicate God's acceptance of the people's blood sacrifices.

What does reconcile mean? It means two former friends make up with each other and are friends again. Never does it mean appeasing God's wrath.

How were the people's individual sacrifices to be made? With humble souls (Leviticus 11:29).

God commanded people to make these bloody sacrifices so they would understand the pain he felt when mankind sinned and left him. God was not obsessed with Sin. He was obsessed with bringing mankind back to him. He was obsessed with reconciling with his children again.

Since Adam's first Sin, God has been running after us crying out, "Come back. Come back to me. I love you. I can protect you. You are my child. Come back."

Why blood? God could have chosen some other symbol to represent his mercy and love. God said in Leviticus 17:11, "For the life of the flesh is in the blood, and I have given it to you on the altar to make atonement [reconciliation to me] for your souls; for it is the blood by reason of the life that makes atonement." So, when we offer life blood to God, we are offering our life to him.

Further, the sacrifice itself is not the important thing. David said in Psalm 51:15-17, "O Lord, open my lips, that my mouth may declare Your praise. For You do not delight in sacrifice, otherwise I would give it; You are not pleased with burnt offering. The sacrifices of God are a broken spirit; a broken and a contrite heart, O God, You will not despise."

By commanding that the people bring their sacrifices to God in humility, they were not satisfying God's wrath. He was helping them experience what he felt as a Father, longing for the return of his children.

Indeed, "God demonstrates His own love toward us, in that while we were yet sinners, Christ died for us (Romans 5:8).

Jim McGuiggan's excellent book, *Dragon Slayer,* explains it eloquently.

"The people to whom he gave this way to peace and life were already thoroughly sinful and yet God went to their rescue. In Exodus 19:4 and 20:2 God describes himself as their deliverer who brought them, not to Mount Sinai, but to himself. He wanted them and it didn't matter that they didn't want him. It was enough that he wanted them…So, when he initiates the atoning system he is not obsessed with Sin at all. He is fulfilling the covenant he made with their fathers because he loved them."

Hey, Satan. You thought you won. You didn't. Your weapon was Sin and Jesus conquered it. Your crown was Death and he knocked it off and trampled it. Right now in heaven there is singing.

> Worthy is the Lamb that was slain
> to receive power and riches
> and wisdom and might
> and honor and glory
> and blessing!
>
> *Revelation 5:12*

Amen!

7~JESUS' LIFE BEFORE HE WAS "BORN"

God had to do some amazing but difficult things to make sure we found the road back to him.

Some people declare, "You claim Jesus was God and God is one. In that case, there was no God before Jesus was born. In fact, when Jesus died on the cross, once again there was no God."

These are good thoughts. They seem to come from logic. But this logic is based on partial knowledge. A person has to look at the facts.

Remember when God spoke to Moses in a burning bush?

Would it have made sense for the other bushes to say, "God never entered us and spoke out of us, so we do not believe God really entered and spoke out of that other bush"? Furthermore, would it make sense to say that before that bush was planted, God did not exist; and after that bush died and was blown away, God did not exist?

We could ask the same questions about the fire. Should all other flames of fire say that, since God did not speak out of them, God did not speak out of that fire either? Should all other flames of fire say that, before that particular flame of fire came into being, God did not exist; and after that particular flame of fire was blown out, God went out of existence?

If your answer to both questions is "No, it wouldn't make

sense," then it does not make sense to deny God put his words in the human body of Jesus just because he didn't put his words in your human body or any other human body.

Jesus Always Existed

John 1:1-3, in the New Testament half of the Bible, it says, Jesus is God: "In the beginning was the Word, and the **Word was with God, and the Word was God**. He was with God in the beginning. Through him all things were made [spoken into existence]; without him nothing was made that has been made."

In John 17:5, Jesus said he had glory with God before the world began.

King Solomon, the son of David, wrote this about Jesus, the Word: "The Lord brought me forth [possessed me] as the **first of his works before his deeds** of old; **I was appointed from eternity**, from the beginning, before the world began. When there were no oceans, I was given birth [brought forth], when there were no springs abounding with water; before the mountains were settled in place, before the hills, I was given birth [brought forth], before he made the earth or its fields or any of the dust of the world" (Proverbs 8:22-26).

"For by him all things were created: things in heaven and on earth, visible and invisible....**He is before all things**, and in him all things hold together. And he is the head of the body, the church; he is the beginning and the firstborn from among the dead" (Colossians 1:16-18). Many verses in the Old Testament including the obvious one ~ Genesis 1:1 ~ say God was the creator of all things.

"Christ Jesus who, being in **very nature God**...made himself nothing, taking the very nature of a servant, being made in human likeness and **being found in appearance as a man**" (Philippians 2:5-8).

"**He appeared in a body**, was vindicated by the Spirit, was seen by angels, was preached among the nations, was believed on in the world, was taken up in glory" (I Timothy 3:16)

"The Son is the radiance of **God's glory and the exact representation of his being**, sustaining all things by his powerful Word. After he provided purification for sins, he sat down at the right hand of the Majesty in heaven ....About the **Son he says, 'Your throne, O God**, will last forever and ever." (Hebrews 1:3, 8).

"He was **foreknown before the foundation of the world,** but has appeared" (I Peter 1:20)

"If anyone acknowledges that Jesus is the Son of God, **God lives in him and he in God**" (I John 4:15).

Well, how can Jesus be eternal and be created too? Your mind has always existed. Your mind is the father of your words. Any time God put his thoughts in Words, that was Jesus before he became Jesus. Any time Jesus spoke in Words, that was Jesus before he became Jesus

Therefore, whenever Jesus said he had to do the will of his Father, he was saying the Words had to obey the Mind.

This also assures us there is only one Word of God.

What Jesus Was

In the New Testament of the Bible (written for Christians), Jesus' apostle John said, "In the beginning was the Word, and the **Word was with God, and the Word was God**. He was with God in the beginning. **The Word became**

flesh and made his dwelling among us. We have seen his glory, the glory of the One and Only [there is only one Word of God] who came from the Father, full of grace and truth" (John 1:1 & 14).

This same apostle wrote in the very last book of the Bible this: "**His name is the Word of God**....On his robe and on his thigh he has this name written: King of kings and Lord of lords" (Revelation 19:13 & 16).

Whenever God Spoke or Appeared, That Was Jesus

When you understand the Word, it helps to understand the Spirit, for we run into the term Holy Son and Holy Spirit both. You have a mind that is the originator of all things you say and do. You have a spirit within you that keeps you alive and animated; when someone dies, we say their spirit left them. And we've already discussed these words.

The part God's Spirit plays is brought out in Genesis 1:1-2 that says, "In the beginning God created the heavens and the earth. Now the earth was formless and empty, darkness was over the surface of the deep, and the Spirit of God was hovering over the waters." This is followed in the rest of the chapter with God saying, "Let there be" and something came into existence.

Here we have God, the Mind, speaking (Jesus the Word) something into existence, and God the Spirit making it happen. (For a further study of the Holy Spirit, I have written *The Holy Spirit: 592 Scriptures Examined* which can be purchased from any book seller or the author's website at https://inspirationsbykatheryn.com.)

8~GOD MATERIALIZED

We have instances when God appeared as a man, but it is always explained that the man was God who had temporarily materialized.

Whenever **God's Angel** is referred to, that is Jesus. He led the Israelites across the wilderness between Egypt and the future Palestine. God told the Israelites, "Pay attention to him and listen to what he says. Do not rebel against him, for he will not forgive your rebellion, since my name is in him….**My angel will go ahead of you**" (Exodus 23:21-23).

Jesus is referred to as God's Angel also in the last book of the Bible, Revelation. "The revelation of Jesus Christ which God gave him…He made it known by sending his angel [Jesus] to his servant John." (See Revelation 1:1-2.)

Furthermore, whenever you read "The Angel of the Lord" (not **an** angel, but **The** Angel), in the Old Testament half of the Bible, that is Jesus. Remember, angel simply means messenger. The passages referring to The Angel always explain that it is God speaking; that is, God the Word speaking ~ Jesus.

Adam & Eve
c. 5000 BC

I think Adam and Eve lived around 100 years in the Garden of Eden because Adam was 130 years old when his third son was born after his first son killed his second son. What was it like in the garden? There is a vivid description in Genesis 1 and 2. What was their relationship with God like there? God walked and talked with them just like Jesus did a few thousand years later.

"They heard the sound of the Lord God walking in the garden in the cool of the day" (Genesis 3:8).

Abraham
2067 BC

When Abraham was ninety-nine years old, "**The Lord appeared** to Abraham....Abraham looked up and saw **three men** standing nearby....He said, 'If I have found favor in your eyes, my Lord, do not pass your servant by....Then **the Lord said**, "I will return to you about this time next year, and Sarah your wife will have a son....Is anything too hard for the Lord?'" (See Genesis 18:1-14.) We see here that Jesus announced the birth of Isaac.

Abraham
2067 BC

There were some cities that were very evil and **God decided** to destroy them completely. "When the men got up to leave, they looked down toward Sodom....Then the **Lord said**, 'Shall I hide from Abraham what I am about to do?'...Then **the Lord said**, 'The outcry against Sodom and Gomorrah is so great and their sin so grievous'...The [three] men turned away and went toward Sodom, but Abraham approached **him** and said: 'Will you sweep away the righteous with the wicked? What if there are fifty righteous people in the city?...

"The **Lord said**, 'If I find fifty righteous people in the city of Sodom, **I will spare** the whole place for heir sake'...When the **Lord had finished speaking** with Abraham, he left and Abraham returned home. The two angels arrived at Sodom in the evening....

"So, when **God destroyed** the cities of the plain, he remembered Abraham." (Genesis 18:16 – 19:1, 29). We see here that Jesus materialized in the form of one of the three men who visited Abraham. When the Lord appeared to Abraham, that was who we would later identify as Jesus.

Abraham
c. 2054 BC

Abraham waited a long time to have a son. When he was finally born, he was a miracle baby, for Abraham was now one hundred years old, and his wife was ninety years old. Later, probably when Isaac was a teenager, God told Abraham to sacrifice his only begotten son to him.

In the Bible account of the sacrifice, it says, "But The Angel of the Lord called out to him from heaven, 'Do not lay a hand on the boy. Now I know that you fear God, because you have not withheld from me your son, your only son' " (Genesis 22:11-12).

Then "The Angel of the Lord called to Abraham from heaven a second time and said, 'I swear by myself, declares the Lord, that, because you have not withheld your son, your only son, I will surely bless you...." (Genesis 22:15-17a).

Hagar
2050 BC

Sarah, the wife of Abraham, could not bear him children. So, according to the custom 4000 years ago, Sarah suggested her husband mate with her Egyptian slave, Hagar, so she could be a surrogate mother for a child for Sarah. But, when Hagar became pregnant, she began acting ugly toward Sarah and taunting her. So Sarah treated Hagar the same way Hagar had treated her, and Hagar ran away.

"**The Angel of the Lord** found her and told her, 'Go back to your mistress and submit to her." He also told her she would have a son and was to name him Ishmael. Hagar replied, "**You are the God** who sees me. I have now seen the One who sees me." (See Genesis 16:9-13.)

Jacob
1906 BC

Years later, Jacob returned home. By this time, he had two wives and twelve sons. He neared his homeland. "So Jacob was left alone, and **the man** wrestled with him till daybreak.....Then the man said, 'Let me go, for it is daybreak.' But Jacob replied, 'I will not let you go unless you bless me....

"Then the man said, Your name will no longer be Jacob, but Israel, because you have struggled with **God** and with men and have overcome....So Jacob called the place Peniel, saying, 'It is because I **saw God face to face**, and yet my life was spared'" (Genesis 32:24-30).

Jacob was about to enter a hostile land that God was giving him. That night, when he wrestled all night, he proved he was a man who could stick with something longer than other men could. He had wrestled with a physical manifestation of God, Jesus.

Moses
1445 BC

Jacob, now called Israel, had a son, Joseph who started out as a slave in Egypt and eventually became next to Pharaoh in importance. He brought his father and brothers to be with him in Egypt. But they did not return home. Joseph apparently lived another thirty years (accounting for the 430 years in some scriptures).

They stayed after Joseph died until the Egyptians turned them into slaves. They were slaves 400 years. Then Moses led them out of their slavery. Moses led these former slaves for forty years.

"With Moses I speak **face to face**, clearly and not in riddles; **he sees the form of the Lord**. Why then were you not afraid to speak against my servant Moses?" (Numbers 12:8).

Balaam
1407 BC

A pagan prophet named Balaam wanted to prophesy against the Israelites. So, **"The Angel of the Lord** stood in the road to oppose him….the Lord opened Balaam's eyes and he saw The Angel of the Lord standing in the road with his sword drawn. So he bowed low and fell face down" (Numbers 22:22, 31).

We know this was not just an ordinary angel because, when an ordinary angel was bowed down to, he said it was wrong. "Then the angel said to me….At this I fell down at this feet to worship him, but he said to me, 'Do not do it! I am a fellow servant" (Revelation 19:9-10). The same thing happened in Revelation 22:8 when John was again told not to bow down before an angel.

Joshua
1406 BC

After Moses died, Joshua took his place. As he led the people near Jericho, Joshua "saw a man standing in front of him with a drawn sword in his hand. The man said, " 'As **commander of the army of the Lord** I have now come.' Then Joshua **fell facedown** to the ground in reverence....The commander of the Lord's army replied, 'Take off your sandals, for the **place where you are standing is holy**' " (Joshua 5:13-15).

Joshua & Israelites
1375 BC

Shortly before Joshua died, **The Angel of the Lord** told the Israelites, "I brought you up out of Egypt and led you into the land I swore to give to your forefathers. I said I will never break **my covenant** with you." Angels did not make covenants with people; only God did.

Gideon
1169 BC

The Israelites settled in their land, but turned from God. Finally Gideon, a supreme judge over Israel was approached by God. "When **The Angel of the Lord** appeared to Gideon, he said, 'The Lord is with you....**The Lord answered**, "I will be with you.' " At the end of their conversation "The Angel of the Lord disappeared. When Gideon realized it was The Angel of the Lord, he exclaimed, 'Ah, sovereign Lord! I have seen the angel of the Lord face to face" (Judges 6:12-16, 21-22).

Samson's Parents
1090 BC

At a time when the Israelites were being ruled by their

enemy because of their sin, **The Angel of the Lord appeared** to Manoah's wife. She told her husband, a man of God came to her who looked like an angel of God, very awesome (Judges 13:3, 6). He later appeared to both Manoah and his wife. Manoah offered to fix him a meal and he turned him down, but said he should prepare a burnt offering to the Lord.

"Then Manoah inquired of **The Angel of the Lord**, 'What is your name, so we may honor you when your word comes true?' He replied, 'Why do you ask my name? It is beyond understanding'." Then Manoah made the burnt offering to the Lord, and "as the flame blazed up from the altar toward heaven, **The Angel of the Lord** ascended in the flame…We are doomed to die, for we have **seen God!**" (Judges 13:12-22).

Elijah
858 BC

The prophet Elijah fled from the evil queen of the Israelites, Jezebel. While he was hiding, **The Angel of the Lord** touched him and told him to eat because he needed to go to the desert of Damascus. He hid in a cave, then "the word of the Lord came to him" (I Kings 19:7-9).

Shadrach, Meshach & Abednego
603 BC

Eventually, God allowed the Israelites to be taken captive to Babylon (today's Iraq). There were three godly Jews among them named Shadrach, Meshach and Abednego. They refused to bow down to a statue, so King Nebuchadnezzar ordered that they be thrown into a fiery furnace.

"Then King Nebuchadnezzar leaped to his feet I

amazement and asked his advisors, 'Weren't there three men that we tied up and threw into the fire...Look! **I see** four men walking around in the fire, unbound and unharmed, and the **fourth looks like a Son of God**' " (Daniel 3:24-25). Then he ordered the three men to come out of the fire, and they did. The fourth "man" disappeared.

9 ~ GOD APPEARED IN OBJECTS

A Whirlwind
c. 2050 BC

We do not know when Job lived. He may have been a contemporary of Abraham because of the length of his life and being valued by possessions instead of money. Job had been very ill, almost to death. His so-called friends came to his home, not to console him, but to blame him for his own illness because of secret sins. Though innocent Job kept his faith through it all, there were still things he did not understand.

"Then the Lord answered Job out of the whirlwind and said, 'Who is this that darkens counsel by words without knowledge?" (Job 38:1,2).

A Stairway
1928 BC

After Jacob deceived his father, Isaac, and got the blessing of his older brother, Esau, he had to flee for his life. While on his way to another country, he had a vision of a stairway [ladder] coming down from heaven with angels ascending and descending on it (Genesis 28:12)

Centuries later, Jesus explained he was that stairway. He said, "Very truly I tell you, you will see 'heaven open, and the angels of God ascending and descending on' the Son of Man" (John 1:51).

A Burning Bush

1446 BC

The Israelites eventually went to Egypt because of a famine, but never returned home. Eventually they were turned into slaves by the Egyptians because they were another nationality that might try to take over their country. They were slaves 400 years. Then God appeared to Moses to tell him to lead them out of slavery. "There **The Angel of the Lord appeared** to him in flames of fire from within a bush....**God called** to him from within the bush...'Do not come any closer,' **God said.** 'Take off your sandals, for the place where you are standing is holy ground.'...**The Lord said,** 'I have indeed seen the misery of my people in Egypt. I have heard them crying out' " (Exodus 3:2-7).

Fire
1446 BC

God freed Abraham's descendants from slavery in Egypt. In 400 years, they had multiplied from 70 of Abraham's great grandchildren to over three million. They needed to be organized. God used Moses to do the leading and organizing. They needed laws. God gave them to Moses over a period of forty days on Mount Sinai.

'The Lord also said to Moses, 'Go to the people and consecrate them today and tomorrow, and let them wash their garments; and let them be ready for the third day, for on the third day the Lord will come down on Mount Sinai in the sight of all the people'....So it came about on the third day, when it was morning, that there were thunder and lightning flashes and a thick cloud upon the mountain and a very loud trumpet sound...Now Mount Sinai was all in smoke because the Lord descended upon it in fire...God answered [Moses] with thunder" (Exodus 19:10,11,16-20).

A Pillar Of Cloud &/Or Fire
1446-1406 BC

The Israelites did not know where they were going because they had been slaves in Egypt 400 years. So God led them. "Then **The Angel of God**, who had been traveling in front of Israel's army, withdrew and went behind them. The **pillar of cloud** also moved from in front and stood behind them, coming between the armies of Egypt and Israel….During the last watch of the night, the **Lord** looked down from the **pillar of fire and cloud** at the Egyptian army and threw it into confusion. (See Exodus 14:19-20, 24.)

Later Jesus appeared in a cloud when Solomon finished building and dedicated the temple in Jerusalem. When the sacred ark (golden chest) of the covenant was brought into the temple and put in the Holy of Holies, as the priests were leaving the building through the Holy Place, a cloud filled the temple, "so that the priests could not stand to minister because of the **cloud**, for the **glory of the Lord** filled the house of the Lord" (I Kings 8:10-11). That cloud, too, was Jesus.

A Pillar Of Cloud
1445 BC

Moses had an older sister, Miriam, and older brother, Aaron. Moses led former slaves for forty years. At one point, his brother and sister resented him being the leader and not them. So, God appeared to them to set them straight.

"Then the Lord came down in a pillar of cloud; he **stood** at the entrance to the tent and summoned Aaron and Miriam. When the two of them stepped forward, he said, "Listen to my words: When there is a prophet among you, I, the Lord, reveal myself to them in visions, I speak to them in dreams. But this is not true of my servant Moses; he is faithful in all my house."

A Rock With Water
1407 BC

The Israelites were in the wilderness after they left Egypt and became thirsty. So, God told Moses and his brother, Aaron (their high priest) to "**speak to that rock** before their eyes and it will pour out its water. You will bring water out of the rock for the community" Exodus 20:8).

In the New Testament half of the Bible, it says they all "drank the same spiritual drink; for they drank from the spiritual rock that accompanied them, and **that rock was Christ**" (I Corinthians 10:4). In fact, Jesus also said he was the water in John 4:14, also in the New Testament half of the Bible.

As an aside, no wonder God was so angry at Moses and Aaron for beating the rock. The rock was Jesus. They were beating Jesus. They did not realize it, but God knew it and we go by God's standards, not man's.

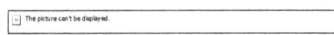

So, we see in the above that the Word of God (later known as Jesus) had a fairly busy life before he was born in the body of Jesus.

Jesus Was The Image Of The Invisible God

The prophet Isaiah wrote that a **child** would be born someday who will be both the Son and the Everlasting Father, and will be **Mighty God** (Isaiah 9:6). In a sense, the Father and son begat each other. They were self-existent.

In America when people see a son looking exactly like his father, they say, "He is a spitting image of his father", meaning the son looks like the father as though he had spit him out of his mouth.

When the angel, Gabriel, appeared to Joseph to explain that Mary was miraculously pregnant, he told Joseph "they will call him Immanuel, which means **"God With Us"**. This had been prophesied centuries earlier when it was said, "Therefore the Lord himself will give you a sign: The virgin will be with child and will give birth to a son, and will call him Immanuel" (Isaiah 7:14).

"For in Christ all the fullness of **Deity dwells in bodily form**, (II Corinthians 5:19)

"He is the **image of the invisible God**, the firstborn over all creation....For God was pleased to have all his fullness dwell in him" (Colossians 1:15, 19).

So, when **God walked with Adam and Eve** in the Garden of Eden (Genesis 3:8), he was in body form. How could these two humans take a walk with a spirit? They were walking with Jesus.

Philippians 2:5-8, explains this: "Your attitude should be the same as that of **Christ Jesus** who, being in very nature God, did not consider **equality with God** something to be grasped, but made himself nothing, taking the very nature of a servant, being made in human likeness. And being in appearance as a man, he humbled himself and became obedient to death—even death on a cross."

So, why did God the Word become the visible image of God the Father by going into the body of a man? Hebrews 2:11-

14, "Both the one who makes men holy [Jesus] and those who are made holy [Jesus' followers, Christians] are the same family. So Jesus is not ashamed to call them brothers.... 'Here am I, and the children God has given me.' Since the children have flesh and blood, he too shared in their humanity so that by his death he might destroy him who holds the power of death—that is, the devil."

10~PROPHECIES OF JESUS FULFILLED IN HIS LIFETIME

(Some of Many)

The road back to God was a long one. God promised he would come to earth and be our king. But how were we to recognize him?

Will he make his entrance as a grown man? Will he be a giant? What about a ring of stars around his head to signify his divine station? Well, if not that, at least a halo.

Will he fling lightning bolts at his mortal enemies? How about riding on the wings of a giant eagle as he goes around spreading his words?

And food. Ah yes, food. Will he eat stones and wash them down with water wrung out from a couple of clouds?

God thought of everything. He put descriptions of what he would say and do once he arrived on earth in the scriptures. He also told of the reaction of both his friends and enemies. These descriptions and reactions are in the form of prophecies.

1. PROPHECY c. 1420 BC - Genesis 22:15,18

"ABRAHAM....through your offspring all nations on earth will be blessed."
FULFILLED - Matthew 1:1
"A record of the genealogy of Jesus Christ the son of

David, the son of ABRAHAM."

2. PROPHECY c. 1000 BC - Psalm 89:3,4,27

"I have made a covenant with my chosen one, I have sworn to DAVID my servant, I will establish your line forever and make your throne firm through all generations....I will also appoint him my firstborn, the most exalted of the kings of the earth."
FULFILLED - John 7:42
"Does not the Scripture say that the Christ will come from DAVID'S family and from Bethlehem, the town where David lived?"

3. PROPHECY c. 530 BC - Daniel 9:24-27

"Seventy 'sevens' [490 years] are decreed for your people and your holy city [Jerusalem] to finish transgression [punishment]....and to anoint [crown] the most holy. Know and understand this: From the issuing of the decree to restore and rebuild Jerusalem until the Anointed One [priest-king], the ruler, comes, there will be seven 'sevens' [49 years] and sixty-two 'sevens' [+434 years = 483 years+]....After the sixty-two 'sevens,' [434 years] the Anointed One [priest-king] will be cut off and will have nothing....He will confirm a covenant with many for one 'seven' [+set of 7 years = 490 years]. In the middle of the 'seven' [3-1/2 years] he will put an end to sacrifice and offering" [sacrifice himself - Hebrews 10:3-5].
FULFILLED
['weeks' = years. 7 days in a week represent years.]
49 years + 434 years = 483 years

BC 457 city walls of Jerusalem rebuilt
AD +26 Jesus, at age 30, began to preach (Luke 3:23)
483 years

\+ 7 years confirm [New] covenant [Testament]
*490 years

*But in middle of the 7 (3-1/2 yrs) will put an end to sacrificing [animal sacrifices]

Jesus preached 3-1/2 years, then was crucified, being the sacrificial Lamb of God (John 1:29, 18:28 & 19:16-18).

After that, sacrificing animals at the Temple became unnecessary (Hebrews 10:3-5).

4. PROPHECY c. 686 BC - Micah 5:2

"But you, BETHLEHEM Ephrathat, though you are small among the clans of Judah, out of you will come for me one who will be ruler over Israel, whose origins are from of old, from ancient times."

FULFILLED - Matthew 2:3-5

"When King Herod heard this, he was disturbed, and all Jerusalem with him. When he had called together all the people's chief priests and teachers of the law, he asked them where the Christ was to be born. 'In BETHLEHEM in Judea,' they replied, 'for this is what the prophet has written.' "

5. PROPHECY c. 600 BC - Jeremiah 31:15

"A voice is heard [way over] in Ramah, mourning and great [loud] weeping. Rachel [Isaac's Wife, Grandmother of 12 Tribes of Israel] WEEPING FOR HER CHILDREN and refusing to be comforted, because her children are no more."

FULFILLED - Matthew 2:16

"When Herod realized that he had been outwitted by the Magi, he was furious, and he gave orders to KILL ALL THE BOYS IN BETHLEHEM AND ITS VICINITY WHO WERE TWO YEARS OLD AND UNDER, in accordance with the time he had learned from the Magi."

6. PROPHECY c. 700 BC - Hosea 11:1

"When Israel was a child, I loved him, and out of EGYPT I called my son."
FULFILLED - Matthew 2:14-15
"So he [Joseph] got up, took the child [Jesus] and his mother [Mary] during the night and left for EGYPT where he stayed until the death of Herod."

7. PROPHECY c. 430 BC - Malachi 3:1

"See, I will SEND MY MESSENGER who will prepare the way before me. Then suddenly, the Lord you are seeking will come to his temple; the messenger of the covenant, whom you desire, will come."
FULFILLED - John 1:19, 29
"Now this was JOHN'S TESTIMONY when the Jews of Jerusalem sent priests and Levites to ask him who he was. He did not fail to confess, but confessed freely, 'I am not the Christ.' The next day John saw Jesus coming toward him and said, 'Lo, the Lamb of God, who takes away the sin of the world!' "

8. PROPHECY c. 700 BC - Isaiah 40:3

"A voice of one calling: 'In the DESERT prepare the way for the Lord, make straight in the WILDERNESS a highway for our God.' "
FULFILLED - Matthew 3:4-5
"John's clothes were made of camel's hair, and he had a leather belt around this waist. His FOOD WAS LOCUSTS AND WILD HONEY. People went out to him from Jerusalem and all Judea and the whole region of the Jordan."

9. PROPHECY c. 700 BC - Isaiah 9:1-2, 7

"In the past he humbled the land of Zebulun and the land of Naphtali. In the future he will honor GALILEE of the Gentiles by the way of the sea, along the Jordan. The people walking in darkness have seen a great light, on those living in the land of the shadow of death, a light has dawned....Of the increase of his government and peace there will be no end."

FULFILLED - Matthew 4:13

"Leaving Nazareth, he went and lived in Capernaum, which was by the lake in the area of Zebulun and Naphtali, to fulfill what was said through the prophet Isaiah, 'Land of Zebulun and land of Nephtali, the way to the sea, along the Jordan, GALILEE of the Gentiles ~ the people living in darkness have seen a great light, on those living in the land of the shadow of death a light has dawned.' From that time on Jesus began to preach, 'Repent, for the kingdom of heaven is near.' "

10. PROPHECY c. 700 BC - Isaiah 35:4-6

"Say to those with fearful hearts, 'Be strong, do not fear; your God will come, he will come with vengeance [against Satan]; with divine retribution he will come to save you.' Then will the eyes of the BLIND be opened, the ears of the DEAF unstopped. Then will the LAME leap like a deer, and the MUTE tongue shout for joy."

FULFILLED - John 20:30-31

"Jesus did many other MIRACULOUS SIGNS in the presence of his disciples, which are not recorded in this book. But these are written that you may believe that Jesus is the Christ, the Son of God, and that by believing you may have life in his name."

11. PROPHECY c. 1000 BC - Psalm 78:2

"I will open my mouth in PARABLES, I will utter hidden things, things from of old."
FULFILLED - Matthew 13:34
"Jesus spoke all these things to the crowd in PARABLES; he did not say anything to them without using a parable. "

12. PROPHECY c. 1000 BC - Psalm 69:8

"I am a stranger to my BROTHERS, an alien to my own mother's sons."
FULFILLED - John 7:5
"For even his own BROTHERS did not believe in him."

13. PROPHECY c. 1000 BC - Psalm 35:19; 69:4; Isaiah 49:7

"Let not those who hate me without reason maliciously wink the eye….Those who HATE ME WITHOUT REASON outnumber the hairs of my head….The Redeemer and Holy One of Israel ~ to him who was despised and abhorred by the nation, to the servant of rulers…the Lord, who is faithful, the Holy One of Israel, who has chosen you."
FULFILLED - John 15:24b-25
"But now they have seen these miracles and yet they have HATED BOTH ME AND MY FATHER. But this is to fulfill what is written in their Law, "They hated me without reason.""

14. PROPHECY c. 450 BC - Zechariah 9:9

"Rejoice greatly, O Daughter of Zion! Shout, Daughter of Jerusalem! See, your king comes to you, righteous and having salvation, gentle and riding on a donkey, on a colt, the FOAL OF A DONKEY."
FULFILLED - Matthew 21:7
"They brought the DONKEY AND THE COLT, placed their cloaks on them, and Jesus sat on them."

15. PROPHECY c. 1000 BC - Psalm 41:9

"Even my CLOSE FRIEND whom I trusted, he who shared my bread, has lifted up his heel AGAINST ME."
FULFILLED - Matthew 10:1-2,4; John 13:21,26
"He called his twelve disciples to him and gave them authority to drive out evil spirits and to heal every disease and sickness. These are the names of the twelve APOSTLES...AND JUDAS Iscariot, who betrayed him....After he had said this, Jesus was troubled in spirit and testified, 'I tell you the truth, one of you is going to BETRAY me...It is the one to whom I will give this piece of bread when I have dipped it in the dish. Then dipping the piece of bread, he gave it to Judas Iscariot....

16. PROPHECY c. 485 BC - Zechariah 11:12

"I told them, 'If you think it best, give me my pay; but if not, keep it." So they paid me THIRTY PIECES OF SILVER."
FULFILLED - Matthew 26:14-15
"Then one of the Twelve ~ the one called Judas Iscariot ~ went to the chief priests and asked, 'What are you willing to give me if I hand him over to you?" So they counted out for him THIRTY SILVER COINS ."

17. PROPHECY c. 485 BC - Zechariah 11:13

"And the Lord said to me, 'Throw it to the potter' ~ the handsome price at which they priced me! So I took the THIRTY PIECES OF SILVER AND THREW THEM INTO THE HOUSE OF THE LORD TO THE POTTER."
FULFILLED Matthew 27:5-7
"So Judas THREW THE MONEY INTO THE TEMPLE and left. Then he went away and hanged himself. The chief priests picked up the coins and said, 'It is against the law to put this into the treasury, since it is blood money.' So they decided to use the money to buy the POTTER'S field as a burial place for foreigners."

18. PROPHECY c. 485 BC - Zechariah 13:7

" 'Awake, O sword, against my shepherd, against the man who is close to me!' declares the Lord Almighty. 'Strike the shepherd, and the SHEEP WILL SCATTER.' "
FULFILLED - Matthew 26:31, 50, 56b
"Then Jesus told them, 'This very night you will all fall away on account of me, for it is written, 'I will strike the shepherd, and the sheep of the flock will be scattered'…. Then the men stepped forward, seized Jesus and arrested him….Then all the DISCIPLES DESERTED HIM AND FLED."

19. PROPHECY c. 700 BC - Isaiah 53:7

"He was oppressed and afflicted; yet he did not open his mouth; he was led like a lamb to the slaughter, and as a sheep before her shearers is silent, so he DID NOT OPEN HIS MOUTH."
FULFILLED - Matthew 27:12
" When he was accused by the chief priests and the elders, he GAVE NO ANSWER."

20. PROPHECY c. 1000 BC – Psalm 2:1-2

"Why do the nations conspire and the peoples plot in vain. The kings of the earth take their stand and the RULERS GATHER TOGETHER AGAINST his Anointed One."
FULFILLED - *Luke 22:66; 23:1, 8*
"At daybreak, the COUNCIL OF THE ELDERS of the people, both the chief priests and teachers of the law, met together and Jesus was led before them....then the whole assembly rose and led him off to [GOVERNOR] Pilate....When he learned that Jesus was under [KING] HEROD'S jurisdiction, he sent him to Herod who was also in Jerusalem at that time.

21. PROPHECY c. 1000 BC - Psalm 69:21

"They put GALL in my food, and gave me vinegar for my thirst."
FULFILLED - Matthew 27:34
"There they offered Jesus wine to drink, mixed with GALL; but after tasting it, he refused to drink it."

22. PROPHECY c. 1000 BC - Psalm 22:18

"They DIVIDE MY GARMENTS among them and cast lots for my clothing."
FULFILLED - Matthew 27:35
"When they had crucified him, they DIVIDED UP HIS CLOTHES by casting lots."

23. PROPHECY c. 700 BC - Isaiah 53:12

"He...made INTERCESSION for the transgressors."
FULFILLED - Luke 23:34
"Jesus said, 'Father, FORGIVE THEM, for they do not

know what they are doing.' "

24. PROPHECY c. 1000 BC - Psalm 22:7-8

"All who see me MOCK me; they hurl INSULTS, shaking their heads; "He trusts in the Lord; LET THE LORD RESCUE HIM. Let him deliver him, since he delights in him."
FULFILLED - Matthew 27:39, 41, 43
"Those who passed by hurled INSULTS at him, shaking their head....In the same way the chief priests, the teachers of the law and the elders MOCKED him....'He trusts in God. LET GOD RESCUE HIM now if he wants him, for he said, "I am the Son of God. " ' "

25. PROPHECY c. 700 BC - Isaiah 53:9

"He was assigned a GRAVE with the WICKED....
FULFILLED - Luke 23:32
"Two other men, both CRIMINALS, were also led out with him to be executed."

26. PROPHECY c. 1000 BC - Psalm 22:1

"MY GOD, MY GOD, WHY HAVE YOU FORSAKEN ME? Why are you so far from saving me, so far from the words of my groaning?"
FULFILLED - Matthew 27:46
"About the tenth hour Jesus cried out in a loud voice, 'Eloi, Eloi lama sabachthani?' ~ which means, 'MY GOD, MY GOD, WHY HAVE YOU FORSAKEN ME?' "

27. PROPHECY c. 1000 BC - Psalm 31:5

"INTO YOUR HANDS I COMMIT MY SPIRIT; redeem me, O Lord, the God of truth."

FULFILLED - Luke 23:46
"Jesus called out with a loud voice, 'Father, INTO YOUR HANDS I COMMIT MY SPIRIT.'"

28. PROPHECY C. 1000 BC - Psalm 34:20

"He protects all his BONES, NOT one of them will be BROKEN."

FULFILLED - John 19:32-33
"The soldiers therefore came and broke the legs of the first man who had been crucified with Jesus, and then those of the other. But when they came to Jesus and found that he was already dead, they did NOT BREAK HIS LEGS."

29. PROPHECY c. 485 BC - Zechariah 12:10

"And I will pour out on the house of David and the inhabitants of Jerusalem a spirit of grace and supplication. They will look on me, the one they have PIERCED."

FULFILLED John 19:34
"Instead, one of the soldiers PIERCED JESUS' side with a spear, bringing a sudden flow of blood and water."

30. PROPHECY c. 700 BC - Isaiah 53:9

"He was...with the RICH IN HIS DEATH, though he had done no violence, nor was any deceit in his mouth."

FULFILLED Matthew 27:57-60
"As evening approached, there came a RICH MAN from Arimathea, named Joseph, who had himself become a disciple of Jesus. Going to Pilate, he asked for Jesus' body, and Pilate ordered that it be given to him. Joseph took the body, wrapped it

in a clean linen cloth, and placed it in his OWN NEW TOMB that he had cut out of the rock."

31. PROPHECY c. 1000 BC - Psalm 45:6, 8

"Your throne, O God, will last for ever and ever; a scepter of justice will be the scepter of your kingdom....All your robes are fragrant with MYRRH AND ALOES and cassia."

FULFILLED - John 19:39

"He was accompanied by Nicodemus, the man who earlier had visited Jesus at night. Nicodemus brought a mixture of MYRRH AND ALOES, about seventy-five pounds. Taking Jesus' body, the two of them wrapped it with the spices, in strips of linen."

32. PROPHECY c. 700 BC - Hosea 6:2

"After two days he will revive us; on the THIRD DAY HE WILL RESTORE US, that we may live in his presence."

FULFILLED Matthew 27:62-64

"The next day, the one after Preparation Day, the chief priests and the Pharisees went to Pilate. 'Sir,' they said, 'we remember that while he was still alive that deceiver said, "After THREE DAYS I WILL RISE AGAIN."

John 19:42 – "Because it was the Jewish DAY OF PREPARATION and since the tomb was nearby, they laid Jesus there.

Luke 23:55-56 – "…saw the tomb and how his body was laid in it. Then they went home…but they RESTED ON THE SABBATH …."

John 20:1,18 – Early on the FIRST DAY OF THE WEEK [3]…Mary Magdalene went to the disciples with the news: 'I have seen the Lord!' "

33. PROPHECY c. 1000 BC - Psalm 16:10-11

"Because you will NOT ABANDON ME TO THE GRAVE, nor will you let your Holy One see decay. You have made known to me the path of life; you will fill me with joy in your presence, with eternal pleasures at your right hand."

FULFILLED Matthew 28:5-6

"The angel said to the women, 'Do not be afraid, for I know that you are looking for Jesus who was CRUCIFIED. He is not here; he HAS RISEN just as he said.' "

11~WHAT DOES JESUS DYING ON THE CROSS HAVE TO DO WITH FORGIVENESS?

Forgiveness is not a simple thing
It has to do with God
taking Satan's power from him.

What Things Are Sin?

Are you a sinner or a very good person to the point of being perfect? Actually, we cannot claim to be both. True, we may not murder, but let's look at the types of sin. There are three types:

1. Bad things we do
2. Bad things we think
3. Good things we do not do

The following comes from the scattered lists in the Bible (Romans 1:29-31; I Corinthians 6:9-1; Galatians 5:19-21; Ephesians 4:31, 541; Philippians 2:3,14; Colossians 3:8-9; I Timothy 1:9-10, 5:13, 6:35; II Timothy 3:2-8; Titus 3:3,9-11; James 3:14-16, 4:1-3, 5:3-6; I Peter 2:1, 4:3, II Peter 2:14-19; Jude 7:8,16; Revelation 21:8).

The easiest way to quickly look at them is in a chart. Here it is.

Bad We Do	Bad We Think	Good We Don't Do
Murder	Greed	Show gratitude
Adultery	Envy	Love good

Homosexuality	Deceit	Acknowledge truth
Gossip	Arrogance	Accept truth
Slander	Without faith	Pay wages
Boasting	Heartlessness	Support family
Prostitution	Hatred	Bear good fruit for God
Idolatry	Jealousy	Lend to someone in need
Stealing	Selfishness	Do good works in private
Drunkenness	Bitterness	Feed hungry
Swindling	Rage	Give thirsty a drink
Witchcraft	Anger	Visit people in prison
Fits of rage	Vanity	Devote self to others
Obscenities	Rebellion	Merciful
Coarse joking	Ungodliness	Contribute to others' needs
Foolish talk	Conceit	Hospitable
Complaining	Evil Suspicions	Do good to enemies
Arguing	Withholding truth	Obey the government
Lying	Loving money	Meet with God's people often
Filthy talk	Pride	Forgive
Law breaking	Without self-control	Gentle
Quarrelsomeness	Rashness	Pray without ceasing
Disobedience to parents	Weak willed	
Opposing truth	Coveting	
Enslaved to passions	Lusting	
Argumentative	Wrong motives	
Quarrelsome	Self-indulgent	
Divisive	Adulterous eyes	
Disorderly	Slavery to sin	
Hoarding wealth	Impatience	
Condemner of innocent	Cowardliness	
Hypocrisy	Vile	
Seducing	Vengeful	
Fault finder		
Grumbler		
Flatterer		
False healing		
Doing good for praise		
Sorcery		

From this list, we can see that everyone sins.

Here are three quick definitions of sin:

1. Trespassing into Satan's jurisdiction.
2. Missing the target of heaven.
3. A fine, a debt.

Spiritual Laws That Cannot Be Broken

ABOUT GOD:

1. It is impossible for God to lie (Hebrews 6:18)
2. It is impossible for God to change (Malachi 3:6; Hebrews 13:8)
3. It is impossible for God to break a promise (Psalm 89:34)
4. It is impossible for God to be pleased with people without faith in him (Hebrews 11:6)
5. It is impossible for God to deny who he is (II Timothy 2:13)
6. It is impossible for God to sleep (Psalm 121:2-3)
7. It is impossible for God to judge wrongly (Ecclesiastes 12:14)
8. It is impossible for God to be tempted to sin (James 1:13)

ABOUT SATAN:

1. It is impossible for Satan to tell the truth. He is the Father of Liars. (John 8:44)
2. It is impossible for Satan to give life. He is the originator of death (John 8:44)
3. It is impossible for Satan to do right. He is the originator of sin (Matthew 13:38)
4.. It is impossible for Satan to forgive. He is the

accuser. (Revelation 12:10)

    5. Satan always tempts people to sin (I Thessalonians 3:5)

    6   He rules over everyone who sins (Ephesians 2:2)

    7.   He is the king of death (Hebrews 2:14)

WHERE DOES GOD LIVE? Heaven.
WHERE DOES SATAN LIVE? Hell

What Happens To Our Soul When We Sin?

1. We obey Satan (Hebrews 2:14)
2. We become separated from God (Isaiah 59:1-2)
3. We earn death (Romans 6:23)
4. The moment we sin, our soul dies (Genesis 2:17)

12~WHAT IS SOUL DEATH?

Technically, the word "Death" means separation. When our body dies, we become separated from our body. When our body dies, we become separated from this earth. When our soul dies, we become separated from God who is Life (Job 33:4; Acts 17:25; John 1:3-4).

There is a "second Death". "But the cowardly, the unbelieving, the vile, the murderers, the sexually immoral, those who practice magic arts, the idolaters and all liars ~ they will be consigned to the fiery lake of burning sulfur. This is the second Death" (Revelation 22:8).

God Cannot Just Forgive Us.

It is more complicated than that. Every time we Sin, our soul dies. That is a terrible predicament to be in. But it is a spiritual law that cannot be broken.

As soon as mankind stepped over the line onto Satan's side, the ghastly trinity took mankind captive. Mankind was doomed to go to hell and there was no intention to free us. Ever.

God Had to Enter Our World

God put a part of himself in the physical world. John 1:1-3, 14 says "In the beginning [of the world] was the Word, and the Word was with God, and the Word was God. He was in the beginning with God. All things came into being through him, and apart from him nothing came into being that has come into being.... And the Word became flesh and dwelt among us, and we saw His glory, glory as of the only begotten from the Father, full of grace and truth"

How could Jesus be created and eternal both? Remember, Jesus was the Word of God placed in a human body. Words are spoken thoughts. Our thoughts have existed as long as we have, even though we create our thoughts.

Here are some other scriptures that state what John 1 said. The church of God was purchased with his own blood (Acts 20:28). God's glory was displayed in the face of Christ (II Corinthians 4:6). God said, "I will live with them and walk with them" (II Corinthians 6:16). Jesus existed in the form of God when he took on the likeness of men (Philippians 2:6).

Jesus was the image of the invisible God, and every part of God dwelled in him (Colossians 1:15-19). Jesus was the exact representation of God's nature (Hebrews 1:2). God was revealed in the flesh (I Timothy 3:16). Our great God and Savior was in Christ Jesus (Titus 2:11-13).

God In Flesh Paid Our Ransom

First, Jesus never Sinned (Hebrews 4:15), so when he died, he proved stronger than sin and so conquered Sin.

Second, he, as part of the fleshly family of mankind, identified with mankind's sins just as many prophets identified with their nations' sins (II Corinthians 5:21; II Peter 2:24), thus conquering Satan, the first sinner.

Third, he died so he could come back to life, thus conquering Death for us (II Timothy 1:10). He freed us from our slavery to Sin, our obedience to Satan, and our inevitable spiral to hell (I Timothy 2:6)

On the cross that day, Jesus, a representative of mankind, a part of the family of man, was still sinless. Sin never tainted him.

Thereby he hurled at Satan what he had been hurling at us. That day, he destroyed the works of Satan.

He Did What's Impossible For Us To Do

He came back to life. In the blink of an eye, Jesus' soul immediately came back to life, and three days later, Jesus' soul re-entered that former body.

Now that the ransom had been paid, Satan, Sin, and Death became powerless to hold mankind captive any longer. Remember, it is impossible for Satan to give life. Satan can only kill. God took over then, and brought the soul of mankind back to life. That is called FORGIVENESS – bringing our soul back to life.

But Not Everyone Is Forgiven

Of course, that does not mean all of mankind will be able to go to heaven. We have to believe God did this for us. If we don't believe it, we cannot accept his atonement, his purifying us of our sins, and we still belong to Satan. We call this belief "faith".

To demonstrate our faith to God, we imitate what that human body did for us: We die to our sinful nature, we are buried in a watery grave, then we come up out of our grave born again, our souls alive (Romans 6:3-4).

Then the rest of our life, we must continue to be loyal to God and try the best we can to do right. He will continue to forgive us, but only if we try not to Sin. We cannot go around having all kinds of fun sinning because God will forgive us; it doesn't work like that. We must keep battling Satan our whole life because Satan wants us back. But if we keep returning to God, he will keep forgiving us. Then we are guaranteed heaven and do not have to wait until the Day of Judgment to know this. (All this is explained in Romans 6.)

13~WHY JESUS HAD TO DIE & COME BACK TO LIFE

Jesus said to her, "'I am the resurrection and the life.
He who believes in me will live,
even though he dies.'"
John 11:25

Death has been swallowed up in victory!
Where, O Death, is your victory?
Where, O Death, is your sting?
Thanks be to God!
He gives us the victory
through our Lord Jesus Christ!
1 Corinthians 15:54b-57

Adam: Physical & Sinful

God did say, 'You must not eat fruit from the tree that is in the middle of the garden, and you must not touch it, or you will DIE'"

To Adam God said, "Because you listened to your wife and ate fruit from the tree about which I commanded you, 'You must not eat from it,' By the sweat of your brow you will eat your food until you return to the ground, since from it you were taken; for dust you are and to dust you will return [DIE]."

And the LORD God said, "The man has now become like one of us, knowing good and evil. He must not be allowed to reach out his hand and take also from the tree of life and eat, and live forever." (Genesis 3:3,19,22)

Mankind ~Physical & Sinful Through Adam

"The wrath of God is being revealed from heaven against all the godlessness and wickedness of people, who suppress the truth by their wickedness. For although they knew God, they neither glorified him as God, nor gave thanks to him, but their thinking became futile and their foolish hearts were darkened.

"They have become filled with every kind of wickedness, evil, greed and depravity. They are full of envy, murder, strife, deceit and malice. They are gossips, slanderers, God-haters, insolent, arrogant and boastful; they invent ways of doing evil; they disobey their parents; they have no understanding, no fidelity, no love, no mercy. Although they know God's righteous decree that those who do such things DESERVE DEATH, they not only continue to do these very things but also approve of those who practice them" (Romans 1:18,21,29-32).

"THERE IS NO ONE RIGHTEOUS, not even one; there is no one who understands; there is no one who seeks God. All have turned away, they have together become worthless; there is no one who does good, not even one. ALL HAVE SINNED AND FALL SHORT of the [sinless] glory of God" (Romans 3:10-12,23).

Abraham, Father Of Faith, Not Works

"What then shall we say that Abraham, our forefather according to the flesh, discovered in this matter? IF, in fact, Abraham was justified by works, he had something to boast about—but not before God. What does Scripture say? 'Abraham believed [had faith in] God, and it was credited to him as righteousness.'

"Now to the one who works, wages are not credited as a gift but as an obligation. However, to the one who does not work but trusts God who justifies the ungodly, their faith is credited as righteousness. Therefore, the promise comes by faith (not works), so that it may be by grace and may be guaranteed to all Abraham's offspring—not only to those who are of the law but also to those who have the faith of Abraham. He is the father of us all.

"The words 'it was credited to him' were written not for him alone, but also for us, to whom God will credit righteousness—for us who believe in him who raised Jesus our Lord from the dead. He was delivered over to Death for our Sins and was raised to life for our justification" (Romans 4:1-5,16,23-25).

Jesus, The Second Adam ~ Spiritual & Sinless

"You see, at just the right time, when we were still powerless, Christ died for the ungodly. Very rarely will anyone die for a righteous person, though for a good person someone might possibly dare to die. But God demonstrates his own love for us in this: While we were still sinners, Christ died (physically and spiritually) for us.

"Therefore, just as Sin entered the world through one man [Adam], and DEATH through SIN, and in this way Death came to all people, because all Sinned

"Nevertheless, DEATH reigned from the time of Adam...even over those who did not Sin by breaking a command, as did Adam, who is a pattern of the one to come.

"But the GIFT is not like the trespass. For if the many died by the trespass of the one man [Adam], how much more did God's grace and the gift that came by the grace of the one man, Jesus Christ, overflow to the many!

"Consequently, just as [Adam's] one trespass resulted in condemnation for all people, so also one righteous act resulted in justification and life for all people. For just as through the disobedience of the one man the many were made sinners, so also through the obedience of the one man [Jesus] the many will be made righteous.

"So that, just as Sin reigned in Death, so also grace might reign through righteousness to bring eternal LIFE through Jesus Christ our Lord" (Romans 5:7-8,12,14,15,18,19,21).

"We implore you on Christ's behalf: Be reconciled to God. God made him [Jesus] who had no Sin to be Sin for us, so that in him we might become the righteousness of God.....To this you were called, because Christ suffered for you, leaving you an example, that you should follow in his steps....He committed no Sin, and no deceit was found in his mouth....He himself [Jesus] bore our Sins" in his body on the cross, so that we might die to Sins and live for righteousness ....by his wounds you have been healed" (I Peter 2:21,22,24). *

"But Christ has indeed been raised from the dead, the first fruits of those who have fallen asleep (died). For since DEATH came through a man [Adam], the resurrection of the dead comes also through a man. For as in Adam all DIE, so in Christ all will be made ALIVE.

"So, it is written: 'The first man Adam became a living being'; the last Adam, a LIFE-giving spirit. The first man was of the dust of the earth; the second man is of heaven. As was the earthly man, so are those who are of the earth; and as is the heavenly man, so also are those who are of heaven. And just as we have borne the image of the earthly man [Adam], so shall we bear the image of the heavenly man [Jesus]" (I Corinthians 15:20-22,45,47-49).

He Bore Our Sins In His Body

God never abandoned Jesus (himself in flesh) at the cross (Matthew 27:46). God abandoned sinful mankind, Jesus representing that sinful mankind, having taken on flesh and joined the family of mankind.

This is a hard saying. If Jesus was sinless, how could he be Sin? The fact is, our Sins did not transfer to him. Jesus was part of the family of mankind. As part of the family of mankind he identified with mankind's Sin.

Daniel, when he read the book of Jeremiah, lamented in Daniel 9:2-6:

" 'I, Daniel, observed in the books the number of the years which was revealed as the word of the Lord to Jeremiah the prophet for the completion of the desolations of Jerusalem, namely, seventy years. So I gave my attention to the Lord God to seek Him by prayer and supplications, with fasting, sackcloth and ashes. I prayed to the Lord my God and confessed and said, "Alas, O Lord, the great and awesome God, who keeps His covenant and lovingkindness for those who love Him and keep His commandments, we have Sinned, committed iniquity, acted wickedly and rebelled, even turning aside from Your commandments and ordinances. Moreover, we have not listened to Your servants the prophets, who spoke in Your name to our kings, our princes, our fathers and all the people of the land."

This is the Daniel who had insisted on worshiping only Jehovah God upon pain of Death. Yet he was identifying with his people.

Later, Ezra did the same thing in 9:5,6,15:

"But at the evening offering I arose from my humiliation, even with my garment and my robe torn, and I fell on my knees and stretched out my hands to the Lord my God; and I said, "O my God, I am ashamed and embarrassed to lift up my face to You, my God, for our iniquities have risen above our heads and our guilt has grown even to the heavens....

"O Lord God of Israel, You are righteous, for we have been left an escaped remnant, as it is this day; behold, we are before You in our guilt, for no one can stand before You because of this."

Ezra, a prophet of God took upon himself the guilt of his people, even though he had not committed their Sins.

An innocent baby whose rebellious city is caught up in war and resulting hunger and homelessness shares in the Sin and suffering of the adults, but it does not take their rebelliousness onto itself.

Although Jesus shared in mankind's fallen state by being in a human body, he did not share our Sins. That day on the cross, Jesus shared in our punishment. He was not our substitute. He was sinless and innocent (Isaiah 53:5). He died for us, but the Sin of all humans was not transferred to him.

And in the process, he destroyed the works of Satan (1 John 3:8).

Mankind Spiritual & Sinless Through Jesus

As part of the family of mankind in flesh, Jesus identified with mankind which was full of Sin.

"Or don't you know that all of us who were baptized into Christ Jesus were baptized into his DEATH? We were therefore buried with him through baptism into DEATH in order that, just as Christ was raised from the dead through the glory of the Father, we too may live a new LIFE.

"For if we have been united with him in a DEATH like his, we will certainly also be united with him in a RESURRECTION like his. For we know that our old self was crucified with him so that the body ruled by Sin might be done away with, that we should no longer be slaves to Sin — because anyone who has died has been set FREE from Sin" (Romans 6:3-11).

> The gospel God promised beforehand
> through his prophets
> in the Holy Scriptures
> regarding his Son who,
> as to his human nature was a descendant of David,
> and who through the [Holy] Spirit of holiness
> was declared with power [miraculously]
> to be the Son of God
> by his resurrection from the dead:
> Jesus Christ our Lord.
> *Romans 1:1b-4*

> Then Death and Hades were thrown into the lake of fire;
> the lake of fire is the second Death.
> *Revelation 20:14*

God had to be manifest in a human body so he could die and come back to life, thus conquering Death for us

14 ~ WHAT ABOUT JESUS' THRONE NEXT TO GOD?

Yes, the Father/Will raised him up to heaven. Then what? The Bible says this:

> Who [is] he that is condemning?
> Christ [is] He that died,
> yea, rather also, was raised up;
> who is also on the right hand of God –
> who also doth intercede for us.
> *Romans 8:34*

First, if Jesus is an intercessor, does that make him a lesser God or another God? In what way is Jesus intercessor? Remember, Jesus is the Image of the invisible God who is Spirit (Colossians 1:15 and John 1:1,2,14). He is also the Words of God (John 1:1). Our body's action and our words intercede between our mind/will and other people who cannot see our mind or will. In the same way, Jesus intercedes between the Mind of God and people who cannot see the Mind of God.

So now, where is Jesus? If Christians believe Jesus died and went to heaven, is he sitting in a lesser throne next to God's greater throne? Does that prove Jesus was not God?

Not Two Thrones

There are not two thrones in heaven ~ one for God and one for Jesus with Jesus' throne sitting on the right side of God's throne.

In the Bible, any time there were two thrones, one at the right side of the king, the Bible says so. When King Solomon's mother came to the throne room, he always ordered her throne to be brought out and set at his right hand. (See I Kings 2:19)

So, Where Is Jesus Sitting?

At the right hand of Jehovah (Psalm 110:1)
At my [God's] right hand (Matthew 22:44)
At the right hand of the Mighty One (Matthew 26:64)
At my [God's] right hand (Mark 12:36)
At the right hand of the Mighty One (Mark 14:62)
At the right hand of God (Mark 16:19)
At my [God's] right hand (Luke 20:42)
At the right hand of the Mighty One (Luke 22:69)
To the right hand of God (Acts 2:33)
At my [God's] right hand (Acts 2:34)
With his [God's] own right hand (Acts 5:31)
At the right hand of God (Acts 7:55)
At the right hand of God (Romans 8:34)
At his [God's] right hand (Ephesians 1:20)
At the right hand of God (Colossians 3:1)
At the right hand of the Majesty in heaven (Hebrews 1:3)
At my [God's] right hand (Hebrews 1:13)
At the right hand of the throne of the Majesty (Hebrews 8:1)
At the right hand of God (Hebrews 10:12)
At the right hand of the throne of God (Hebrews 12:2)
At God's right hand (I Peter 3:22)

The word "at" in the original Greek of the New Testament is *en*. This word is translated 114 times as "among", 129 times as "with", 302 times as "at", 1863 times as "ON". Therefore, using "ON the right hand of God" we have a whole new understanding and a whole new question.

What Is The Right Hand Of God?

Created the world ~ 2 scriptures.
Is his righteousness ~ 3 scriptures.
Is his loving kindness ~ 2 scriptures.
Cares for his people ~ 15 scriptures
Conquers his people's enemies ~ 18 scriptures
Is the Savior – 15 scriptures

Therefore, when Jesus came back to life and ascended to heaven, he took his place as our Savior who conquered our greatest enemies ~ Satan and Death.

Where Is He In Relation To The Throne Of God?

Remember, Jesus was the Word of God that we humans could see and hear physically. So, when he returned to heaven, he still was the Word of God. He was not a sub-God. Remember John 1? He was just as much God as your words are you.

The Bible explains it clearly.

"But about THE SON he says, YOUR THRONE, O GODE, will last for ever and ever" (Hebrews 1:8).

"I am the Living One; I was dead, and now look, I am alive for ever and ever….To the one who is victorious, I will give the right to sit with me on my throne, just as I was victorious and sat down WITH MY FATHER on his throne. (Revelation 1:18, 3:21).

"These in white robes...have washed their robes and made them white in the blood of the Lamb. Therefore, they are before the throne of God and serve him day and night in his temple; and he who sits on the throne will shelter them with his presence. 'Never again will they hunger; never again will they thirst. The sun will not beat down on them,' nor any scorching heat. For the LAMB [Jesus] AT THE CENTER OF THE THRONE will be their shepherd; 'he will lead them to springs of living water. And God will wipe away every tear from their eyes.'" (Revelation 7:13-17).

Jesus is not and never was an inferior God on a separate throne. He is God the Word and sits on God's throne.

Ephesians 4:10 says that Jesus ascended far above the heavens; that is, far above the universe. He ascended to where God was because Jesus was God.

15~WHY ARE WE HERE?-1

Now we have come full circle on why the world was created. Remember, Ephesians 3:9-12 says, "Bring to light what is the administration of the mystery [being saved from Satan, Sin, and Death and forgiven] which for ages has been hidden in God who created all things; so that the manifold wisdom of God might now be made known THROUGH THE CHURCH to the rulers and the authorities in the heavenly [spiritual] places. This was in accordance with the **eternal purpose which He carried out in Christ Jesus** our Lord in who we have boldness and confident ACCESS through faith in him."

For God to Have Sons & Daughters

"For it was fitting for Him for whom are all things, and through whom are all things, in bringing many sons to glory, to perfect the author of their salvation through suffering. For both He who sanctifies and those who are sanctified are all from one another; for which reason He is not ashamed to call them brethren saying, 'I will proclaim Your name to My brethren'....Therefore, He **had to be** made like His brethren in all things" (Hebrews 2:10-12a; 17a).

The Word in flesh made it possible for us to be sons and daughters of the Father (II Corinthians 6:18). "When the fullness of the time came, God sent forth His Son, born of a woman, born under the Law, so that He might redeem [ransom] those who were under the Law that we might receive the adoption as sons. Because you are sons, God has sent forth the Spirit of His Son into our hearts crying, 'Abba! Father!' Therefore, you are no longer a slave, but a son; and if a son, then an heir through God" (Galatians 4:4-7).

Now, Jesus was ready to hand the reins over to his

brothers and sisters. But why? Why didn't he end the world right then and there?

To Rescue As Many As Possible

Not everyone takes advantage of what Jesus did to free them. If people do not believe it, they will just continue to hang around Satan and follow his orders voluntarily. The apostle Peter said, "The Lord is not slow about His promise, as some count slowness, but is patient toward you, not wishing for any to perish but for all to come to repentance" (II Peter 3:9).

The Word of God said just before leaving earth, "Go, therefore and make disciples of all the nations, baptizing them in the name of the Father [Will], and the Son [Word] and the Holy Spirit [Life Giver], teaching them to observe all that I commanded you; and lo, I am with you always, even to the end of the age [world]."

When will the end of the world come? Many people have taken different symbolic numbers in the Bible and given it a date. Such arrogance! Jesus, himself, said he did not know (Matthew 24:36), so who would dare declare himself superior to Jesus?

We Christians were created in Christ Jesus according to his purpose (Romans 8:28) and for good works which God prepared beforehand (Ephesians 2:10). What good works did God prepare for us and how are we to do them?

First, we are to take on the whole armor of God ~ things that drive Satan and his followers nuts: truth, righteousness, the Gospel of Peace, faith, hope, salvation, the Word of God (Ephesians 6:10-17; I Thessalonians 4:17)).

To Strengthen The Heavenly Spirit World

We are to be prayer warriors because the battle is still going on in the spirit world. As Paul said, "Our struggle is not against flesh and blood, but against the rulers, against the powers, against the world forces of this darkness, against the spiritual forces of wickedness in the heavenly [spiritual] places" (Ephesians 6:12).

Our prayers are powerful. In Daniel 10, the prophet prayed and fasted in mourning over the Sins of his people for three weeks ~ twenty-one days (Daniel 10:2). Three days later a "man" appeared to Daniel with the description of glorified Jesus in Revelation 1:13, but some believe it was Gabriel who had previously appeared to Daniel in chapter 10.

Regardless, he said that God had heard his words the whole twenty-one days, but the prince of Persia (Satan's angel assigned to Persia) "was withstanding me for twenty-one days; then behold, Michael, one of the chief princes [angels] came to help me" (Daniel 10:13). Did Daniel's prayers give strength to angels in the other world?

Yes, we are more powerful than the angels. I Corinthians 6:3a says, "Do you not know that we will judge angels?"

To Reveal The Mystery To The Spirit World

Romans 16:20 says we are crushing Satan, thus working with God to fulfil the promise at the beginning in Genesis 3:15: "I will put enmity between you [Satan] and the woman, and between your seed and her seed. He shall bruise you on the head and you shall bruise him on the heel."

Satan wants to prove everyone is ultimately evil. Just read about righteous Job and all the things Satan accused him of in Job 1. Satan does not comprehend forgiveness and mercy. Satan wants to convince us that traits like mercy and love are weak and ridiculous. He wants to prove his way will bring us glory by making self number one.

Satan has access to God, periodically goes to heaven, and is always falling down. He didn't stay around heaven long when he accused Job and Job refused to blame God for his problems. He was constantly falling when Jesus sent out his seventy-two on a preaching tour (Luke 10:18).

Satan also has access to man. Check this list:

To Eve (Genesis 3:1-4)
To David (I Chronicles 21:1)
To Job (Job 1:6-12)
To Joshua the High Priest Zechariah 3:1-2
To Jesus (Matthew 4:1-11)
To hearers of the Word (Matthew 13:19,38,39)
To the sick (Mark 3:22-26; Luke 13:16)
To Peter (Luke 22:31)
To Judas (John 13:2,27)
To Ananias (Acts 5:3)
To Elymas (Acts 13:9,10)
To the church at Corinth (II Corinthians 2:11; 4:4; 11:3; 12:7)
To the church at Ephesus (Ephesians 2:2; 4:27; 6:11-16)
To the church at Colossae (Colossians 1:13; 2:15)
To Paul (I Thessalonians 2:18; 3:5)
To Hymenaeus and Alexander (I Timothy 1:20)
To Elders (I Timothy 3:6,7; 5:15)

He wants people to follow his "wisdom" that is "from below" (James 3:14,15) like jealousy, selfish ambition, arrogance, and lying. He wants us to be haughty (Romans 12:16) and "wise in our own conceits" (Proverbs 26:12), our own pride.

By example, Satan convinces people to accuse each other and refuse to forgive because he is the Accuser (Revelation 12:10). Satan convinces people to lie because he is the Father of Lies (John 8:44). Satan puts his spirit of disobedience in people (Ephesians 2:2).

In revealing the mystery, the church is to reveal the wisdom of God (Ephesians 3:9).

Wisdom from God is pure, peaceable, gentle, easy to be entreated, merciful, full of good works (James 3:17) ~ things that Satan and his angels do not understand; they are completely foreign to them.

To Explain Things To Angels

I Peter 1:10-12 says, "Concerning this salvation.… Even angels long to look into these things."

There is no plan of salvation for angels. There is no plan to forgive angels. Angels need to know why humans can be forgiven and why humans will be placed above them.

Hebrews 1:14 says God's angels are servants of the saved. I Corinthians 6:3 says we will judge angels. Angels need to understand why they must be our servants and why we will judge them someday.

Further, angels are used to being the highest level of beings in heaven. But God has set us up so we will be higher than them. Revelation 5:10 says humans reign right now in the kingdom as priests and kings. This will continue in heaven (Revelation 3:21).

16 ~ WHY ARE WE HERE?-II

To Strengthen Us

Weak people go with the flow. When it's easy to steal when a clerk isn't looking, we steal. When it covers something bad we did, we lie. When we want to get drunk, we do so and then drive. When we can stop kids from bickering, we beat them because it's quicker. When we want to sleep in on a work day, we speed to get to work. When we want someone else's job, we just start a rumor.

Weak people do like Satan and Adam. Weak people take shortcuts that only lead to a wilderness of darkness. Adam and Eve wanted to be as smart as God, so stole the fruit,

Weak people make excuses for every wrong. It's always, "I had to because," or "The devil made me do it," or "It was only a little Sin."

Weak people are selfish and complain about everything they don't like and is unfair to them. They often complain about the results of trying to break the laws of nature. If a car slams into another car and someone dies, they blame God for not turning the cars into cotton so no one would be hurt. They complain that other people are mean to them. They complain because the want everything to be perfect like in heaven and right now.

Weak people have no time for God because he is not entertaining, uses up time they could be at a ball game, demands money we need to buy a second motorcycle. Weak people are out for number one. As a result, weak people Sin and don't care and weak people go to hell.

We were born to die here on earth so we can move on to our eternal world where there is no Sin. But doing so is not for the faint of heart. Early in this book, we discussed how difficult times leads to spiritual muscles like lifting heavy weights leads to physical muscles.

Weak people blame God and desert him. Weak people give Satan more power than he has. Weak people cannot accept chastisement.

Hebrews 12:5-8 says, "My son, do not regard lightly the discipline of the Lord, Nor faint when you are reproved by Him; For those whom the Lord loves He disciplines, And He scourges every son whom He receives".... But if you are without discipline, of which all have become partakers, then you are illegitimate children and not sons.

Do you see bad people out there getting richer and more powerful and popular and everything in their life is perfect? Consider the above scripture. And consider when God took on weak flesh, then became weak even by human standards.

For indeed He was crucified because of weakness, yet He lives because of the power of God. For we also are weak in Him, yet we will live with Him because of the power of God directed toward you (II Corinthians 13:4).

Satan is powerful, true. He is prince of this world (John 12:31). the god of this world (II Corinthians 4:4). and prince of the powers of the air (John 16:11).

But Satan is not as powerful as he has fooled us into believing. He cannot interfere with your salvation in the following ways. Satan is only allowed to strengthen your faith. Let us look at Job 1-3 to learn all the things Satan is not.

First, let us look at what Satan was doing at the beginning of this account. He was reporting in to God. God asked him what he had been doing and Satan told him he had been walking to and fro upon the earth and walking back and forth on it.

Satan is Not Omniscient

Then, God brought up the faithfulness of Job and Satan took the bait. Satan, the perpetual accuser, accused Job of being a hypocrite. How did he know that? Did he climb inside the mind of Job? If he had, he would have known his accusations were not accurate. Turns out, after all the following devastating events, he had not known Job's mind at all.

THEREFORE, Satan cannot climb inside your mind and know what you are thinking either. Also, he cannot climb inside your mind and give you the excuse "The devil made me do it." He does not have that power.

Satan is Not Omnipotent

After accusing Job of being a hypocrite, Satan decided to prove it. But he didn't have the power to do all the bad things he wanted to do to Job for being good. So he told God, "Put put forth Your hand now and touch all that he has; he will surely curse You to Your face."

Why didn't Satan stretch out his own hand and touch all Job had? Because he didn't have the power to. He told God, "You do it." God parried it and gave Satan the permission and power to do it. God knew it would just make Job stronger and decided to let Satan be the instrument to make it happen and make a fool of himself.

So, since Satan had to leave heaven to do his dirty deed, we see he is not omnipresent or omniscient. He made storms come rise up and blow one of his children's houses away. But he did it only with God's permission.

So, did Job cave like Satan said he would?

Jeremiah 14:22 says, "Are there any among the idols of the nations who give rain? Or can the heavens grant showers? Is it not You, O Lord our God? Therefore we hope in You, For You are the one who has done all these things."

THEREFORE, Satan does not cause wind or rain or lightning or anything else in the weather. Further, he does not curse houses and make them fall down.

"Then Job arose and tore his robe and shaved his head, and he fell to the ground and worshiped. He said, 'Naked I came from my mother's womb, and naked I shall return there. The Lord gave and the Lord has taken away. Blessed be the name of the Lord.' Through all this Job did not Sin nor did he blame God." (Job 1:20-22)

Notice who Job said caused these things to happen: God. He knew God had his reasons.

Then in 42:11 of Job, his relatives came "and comforted him for all the adversities that the Lord had brought on him. And each one gave him one piece of money, and each a ring of gold." Then God blessed Job with far more than what he had before.

Through all the disasters, God was defending Job and bragging on him. Satan accused him of hypocrisy, so God sent Satan to bring bad things on him. It only proved how good Job was and that he would only grow stronger. Then God blessed him even more.

The apostle Paul was stricken, as related in II Corinthians 12, "Because of the surpassing greatness of the revelations, for this reason, to keep me from exalting myself, there was given me a thorn in the flesh, a messenger of Satan to torment me—to keep me from exalting myself!"

Who gave this messenger of Satan permission to do this? "Concerning this I implored the Lord three times that it might leave me. And He has said to me, "My grace is sufficient for you..."

Was God playing with Paul? No, God sent the messenger of Satan to attack Paul to make him stronger: "...for power is perfected in weakness." Most gladly, therefore, I will rather boast about my weaknesses, so that the power of Christ may dwell in me. Therefore I am well content with weaknesses, with insults, with distresses, with persecutions, with difficulties, for Christ's sake; **for when I am weak, then I am strong."**

THEREFORE, only God can turn sickness and handicaps into victory.

Nor Does He Have Power Over Nations

In Isaiah 10:5, God said, "Woe to Assyria, the rod of My anger and the staff in whose hands is My indignation. I send it against a godless nation."

But the bad nation did not realize it was doing God's work to chastise. "Yet it [Assyria] does not so intend, Nor does it plan so in its heart, but rather it is its purpose to destroy and to cut off many nations" (v. 7).

Then God punished the punisher. ""I will punish the fruit of the arrogant heart of the king of Assyria and the pomp of his haughtiness" (v. 12).

"By the power of my hand and by my wisdom I did this, for I have understanding; and I removed the boundaries of the peoples and plundered their treasures, and like a mighty man I brought down their inhabitants" (v. 13).

Why? God uses bad nations to chastise good nations gone bad in order to bring them back to himself. As a loving Father, God chastises his children because he loves them and wants only good for them if they will just return to him and his protection.

. "And we know that all things work together for good to those who love the Lord and are called according to his purpose" (Romans 8:28).

"…seated Jesus at His right hand in the heavenly places far above all rule and authority and power and dominion, and every name that is named, not only in this age but also in the one to come. 22 And He put all things in subjection under His feet" (Ephesians 1:20-22).

THEREFORE, Satan does not have enough power to control nations. So whatever is happening in your nation has a purpose. Don't be afraid or discouraged.

Why Do We Need Strengthening?

We need to stay strong to resist criticizing God when he chastises us. God is trying to change our lives that take us closer to him and his protection from hell.

We need to stay strong for what God may have planned for us in heaven.

God does not condone idleness. Therefore, in heaven we will not be idle. What will we be doing? Perhaps the verse in Revelation above and Jesus parable of the minas and ties explains it: "The first one came and said, 'Sir, your mina has earned ten more.' "'Well done, my good servant!' his master replied. 'Because you have been trustworthy in a very small matter, take charge of ten cities.' "The second came and said, 'Sir, your mina has earned five more.' "His master answered, 'You take charge of five cities.' (Luke 19:12-27)

Perhaps, just perhaps ~ and I'm guessing here ~ one of the works God planned for us since the beginning (Ephesians 2:10) was to put each one of us in charge of one of the two trillion galaxies out there. The angels may wonder why they are not put in charge. However, to be put in charge of anything, a leader must be tried so that they will attribute all good things to God and will not give in and do a half-hearted job. On earth, we are being tested and tried. On earth, every time we go through difficulties and refuse to blame God, we pass the test. Every time something wonderful happens and we do not take the credit for it but rather give God the glory, we pass the test.

17~HOW HARD IS IT?

We have already discussed God chastising us by sending us bad things in our life in order to strengthen our spiritual muscles.

Jesus called Satan the prince of this world (John 12:31). Paul called him the god of this world (II Corinthians 4:4). But he is this only with God's permission.

God keeps turning the tables on Satan. Every time Satan thinks he has won, he loses. Satan thinks he controls the earth, but God is using him. Satan is toughening us up for whatever future plans God has for us in heaven. For now, we have to toughen up our spiritual muscles for the works he has planned for us to do.

We are at war with Satan. We are taking part in a campaign of sabotage against Satan who controls the earth. God arrived behind enemy lines disguised as a man and was only recognized by us, the "freedom fighters".

"Fight the good fight, keeping faith and a good conscience which some have rejected and suffered shipwreck in regard to their faith" (I Timothy 1:18,19). "Fight the good fight of faith; take hold of the eternal life to which you were called" (I Timothy 6:12a). "Experience the same conflict which you saw in me" (Philippians 1:30). "I box in such a way as not beating the air" (I Corinthians 9:26).

We, as workers together with God (II Corinthians 6:1) and soldiers fighting evil, are to stand strong, and keep our armor on at all times so we can extinguish all the flaming arrows of Satan (Ephesians 6:10-17).

Satan convinces people we are the enemy. We must convince them to lay down their arms and surrender to Jesus, realizing they cannot obtain happiness while listening to Satan's lies.

We Don't Like Rules

Satan didn't like rules and he convinced Eve to not like rules either. Many people reject Christianity because they don't like all the rules. That's like rejecting physicians' orders to eat right, exercise, take vitamins, take certain medications when needed. God's rules are not to hold us down. They are to hold Satan off.

Every one of the rules God gives us is to keep us away from Satan. There are horror books and movies and TV shows showing people being threatened by sadistic serial killers. What are the victims doing? They are screaming and begging, "Please, please. Don't kill me. I'll do anything. Just tell me what you want me to do. Only don't kill me. Please don't kill me." Then more screaming. People will do this to escape physical Death.

Why wouldn't people want to do the few rules God gives us to keep Satan from forever killing our souls?

But, mankind has a hard time thinking of their spirits, their souls, that they cannot see. So, people continue to complain about the few rules of God.

We Think We're Good Enough

On the other hand, there are those who try to be so good, God will have no choice but to take them into heaven. That's impossible! It only takes one Sin to be a sinner and God cannot co-exist with Sin. These people, too, need to lay down their arms of self-absorption and surrender. Satan has them in his custody. They can only be freed by the ransom paid by God in flesh.

We are to stop at nothing to get to these people and wake them up, no matter what they do to us. We are to go where we are needed or stay and protect the home front. We are to persist.

The following is from II Corinthians 6:4b-10. Read each line carefully. This is what the church is to be doing.

> As servants of God
> In much endurance.
> In afflictions, hardships, distress.
> In beatings, imprisonments, tumults.
> In labors, sleeplessness, hunger.
> In purity and knowledge.
> In patience, kindness, genuine love.
> In the Word of truth.
> In the power of God.
>
> By the weapons of righteousness
> For the right hand and the left.
> By glory and dishonor,
> By evil report and good report.
> Regarded as deceivers yet true,
> As unknown, yet well-known.
>
> As dying, yet, behold, we live.
> As punished yet not put to Death.
> As sorrowful, yet always rejoicing.
> As poor, yet making many rich.
> As having nothing yet possessing all things.

How long must we go through this? Until the fullness of time.

We Don't Get The Big Picture

When our life is going in the wrong direction and we cannot figure out why, we complain and think God is not answering our prayers.

Complaining is a sin. It tells God he doesn't know what he is doing. It insults God.

God said, "How long shall I bear with this evil congregation who are grumbling against Me? I have heard the complaints of the sons of Israel, which they are making against Me. Say to them, 'As I live,' says the Lord, 'just as you have spoken in My hearing, so I will surely do to you' (Numbers 14:27-30).

"Jesus answered and said to them, "Do not grumble among yourselves" (John 6:43).

"Do all things without grumbling or disputing" (Philippians 2:14).

Joseph Sold As A Slave

Joseph, a great grandson of Abraham. He was his father Jacob's (AKA Israel's) favorite son. His jealous brothers sold him to traders in a caravan for twenty pieces of silver and was taken to Egypt to be resold as a slave. (Genesis 37:36) He was 17 years old.

Some time later, his master's wife tried to seduce him. He refused to dishonor God that way. She was so enraged, she lied to her husband who then imprisoned him. (Genesis 39).

He was released from prison at age 30. Then, suddenly, this ex-con was elevated to prime minister of Egypt. '"You will be in charge of my court, and all my people will take orders from you. Only I, sitting on my throne, will have a rank higher than yours.'

"Pharaoh said to Joseph, 'I hereby put you in charge of the entire land of Egypt.' Then Pharaoh removed his signet ring from his hand and placed it on Joseph's finger. He dressed him in fine linen clothing and hung a gold chain around his neck. Then he had Joseph ride in the chariot reserved for his second-in-command. And wherever Joseph went, the command was shouted, "Kneel down!" So Pharaoh put Joseph in charge of all Egypt. And Pharaoh said to him, "I am Pharaoh, but no one will lift a hand or foot in the entire land of Egypt without your approval." (Genesis 41:41-44)

Then, after seven years of bumper crops plus two years of famine, his brothers showed up in Egypt for food, not recognizing him. When Joseph revealed his identity to them, they were afraid he was going to kill them. Instead, he said,

"I am Joseph, your brother, whom you sold into slavery in Egypt. But don't be upset, and don't be angry with yourselves for selling me to this place. It was God who sent me here ahead of you to preserve your lives. This famine that has ravaged the land for two years will last five more years, and there will be neither plowing nor harvesting. God has sent me ahead of you to keep you and your families alive and to preserve many survivors. So it was God who sent me here, not you! (Genesis 45:5-).

At age 38, Joseph finally understood why he had gone through all those terrible things for the past twenty years.

But backtracking, what was Joseph's attitude all those years he was falsely imprisoned? Did he rant and rave and swear at the prison guards and get into fights with the other inmates?

"So he took Joseph and threw him into the prison where the king's prisoners were held, and there he remained. But the Lord was with Joseph in the prison and showed him his faithful love. And the Lord made Joseph a favorite with the prison warden. Before long, the warden put Joseph in charge of all the other prisoners and over everything that happened in the prison. The warden had no more worries, because Joseph took care of everything. The Lord was with him and caused everything he did to succeed" (Genesis 20-23).

400-Year Slavery Of Jews

Genesis 46:26-27 ~ All the persons belonging to Jacob, who came to Egypt, his direct descendants, not including the wives of Jacob's sons, were sixty-six persons in all, 27 and the sons of Joseph, who were born to him in Egypt were two; all the persons of the house of Jacob, who came to Egypt, were **70.**"

Apparently Joseph lived another thirty years after his father and brothers joined him in Egypt. That would have made Joseph close to 70 years of age when he died. Then trouble began. The Egyptians resented these foreigners in their presence and gradually enslaved them all. Thousands were born in slavery.

God told Abraham his descendants would be **slaves** for 400 years in Genesis 15:13.

Exodus 12:40-41 ~ "Now the length of time the Israelite people **lived in** Egypt[was 430 years. At the end of the 430 years, to the very day, all the Lord's divisions left Egypt."

Exodus 12:37 ~ "Now the sons of Israel journeyed from Rameses to Succoth, about 600,000 men on foot, aside from children."

Do you see this? God promised Abraham he would become the father of a great nation. But it would take time. Abraham's grandson, Jacob (AKA Israel) entered Egypt with a family of 70. They had 30 years of peace with Joseph, then 400 years of slavery. Under "protective custody", by the end of that time, there were 600,000 men, + c. 600,000 wives + average of 2 children per couple. That's at least 2,000,000 people. Now they were big enough to become the nation God promised to Abraham. In fact, their first stop was Mount Sinai where God gave Moses the national rules of organization and laws of conduct.

Do you think the slaves during those centuries died thinking their prayers for freedom and respect had not been answered? Yes. They could not see the big picture.

Moses Exiled

Moses was born some 80 years before the Jews were freed, though no one at the time knew that. Though Pharaoh ordered all boy babies drowned, Moses was saved by a princess of Egypt and raised by her. He was educated, given luxuries and servants and lived in the palace. He also knew he was Jewish by nationality.

"Moses was educated in all the wisdom of the Egyptians and was powerful in speech and action. When Moses was 40 years old, he decided to visit his own people, the Israelites. He saw one of them being mistreated by an Egyptian, so he went to his defense and avenged him by killing the Egyptian" (Acts 7:23-24).

When word spread all over Egypt that the prince killed an Egyptian to save a lowly slave, Moses fled for his life and lived in exile in the desert another 40 forty years. He was doomed to live, not as a prince but as a smelly shepherd; not in a palace but in a tent.

Then God spoke to Moses and sent him back to Egypt where there were still those who sought his life. It is possible the Pharaoh was his step-brother. Against all odds including Pharaoh's army, Moses led millions of slaves out of the country.

It had been 80 years since his birth when his mother slipped him into a little boat in a river full of crocodiles, happened to have been saved by a princes, happened to be educated in writing and the military and astronomy, happened to kill someone, happened to flee to the desert that kept him alive for four decades.

Little did Moses dream through all those unpredictable years of twists and turns he was being groomed to be one of the greatest leaders and prophets in world history.

Deuteronomy 4:10 ~ "Since that time, no prophet has risen in Israel like Moses, whom the LORD knew face to face."

Naomi In A Famine

Naomi lived in Bethlehem around 1300 BC. There was a famine and it drove her, her husband, and their two sons from Bethlehem to a foreign country. While there, her husband died.

Her sons married and then died. What pain. There she was a widow in a strange land. And her daughters-in-law were now widows too. Three painful funerals. Three events asking God through tears, why. Three struggling to survive as widows and no one to support them.

Naomi decided to go home to Bethlehem. One of her

daughters-in-law insisted on going with her even though it was a strange land with strange customs.

When they got to Bethlehem, Ruth had to go to work to support them. With no other skills (she'd probably been "just a house wife"), she went to a field to pick grain in the hot sun all day.

But it wasn't just any field. God led this young widow to the field of a rich man named Boaz. He fell in love with her and she him. They were married.

And then...and then...Ruth, the former bereaved widow, became the great grandmother of King David and ancestress of Jesus. (All this is found in the book of Ruth in the Old Testament of the Bible.)

If Ruth hadn't suffered so many things, then left her homeland, then picked just the right field without becoming bitter, David the "sweet psalmist of Israel" would never have been born.

70-Year Babylon Captivity

Jeremiah 25:8-11 declares, "Therefore thus says the Lord of hosts: Because you have not obeyed my words, I am going to send for all the tribes of the north, says the Lord, even for King Nebuchadnezzar of Babylon, my servant, and I will bring them against this land and its inhabitants....This whole land shall become a ruin and a waste, and these nations shall serve the king of Babylon seventy years.

For 70 years God's people worked through why they were there. It didn't seem fair that their city had been burned to the ground and they had to become slaves. Where was God? He was supposed to protect them.

Jeremiah 7:3-6 says, "But I will be merciful only if you stop your evil thoughts and deeds and start treating each other with justice; only if you stop exploiting foreigners, orphans, and widows; only if you stop your murdering; and only if you stop harming yourselves by worshiping idols."

They weren't ready to admit any guilt or make any changes to their lives. It took time. They were stubborn and refused to admit any of it was their fault. Finally, they swallowed their pride, admitted they had been wrong, and decided to return to God who would protect them from hell and take them to heaven some day. What was the result? They were freed by the Persians, returned home, rebuilt the temple, and returned to worshipping God instead of idols. God had chastised them and when they admitted their wrongs, they were willing to change.

Paul, The Terrorist

This man, Paul, lived during the time of Jesus and hated him. His hatred continued even after Jesus died. He transferred his hatred to people who loved Jesus. He was obsessed to the point that he went house to house hunting down down Christians, probably with temple guards. He hauled them into prison, tortured them to get them to renounce Jesus, then killed them. (Acts 8:3)

Paul himself said, "I was a violent man" (I Timothy 1:12).

Explaining details of his life he said, "Indeed, I myself thought I must do many things contrary to the name of Jesus of Nazareth. This I also did in Jerusalem, and many of the saints I shut up in prison, having received authority from the chief priests; and when they were put to Death, I cast my vote against them . And I punished them often in every synagogue and compelled them to blaspheme; and being exceedingly enraged against them, I persecuted them even to foreign cities" (Acts 26:9-11).

What about all those Christians who prayed to escape being imprisoned? What about all those Christians who who prayed to not be tortured in agony by this man? What about all those families who mourned their loved ones who had been killed by Paul and asked God, Why was all these terrible things happening to them?

It took a lot to break a crazed man like Paul. What kind of toll was it making on this man so full of hatred? Jesus had to personally appear to him and make him blind to knock all the wind out of Paul and get him to stop. (Acts 22:6-11)

And, even after he became a turncoat and believed in Jesus after all, when he went to Jerusalem, he tried to associate with Jesus' followers, "but they were all afraid of him, not believing that he was a disciple" (Acts 9:26.)

Probably hundreds were tortured and killed by Paul, not only to save their own souls, but also Paul's. Of course, they died not knowing that. And then the agony Paul went through when he was told by God himself, "You're wrong."

It took a lot of aguish by a lot of people to save this one man and they didn't even know it at the time. No one knew at the time that one day this terrorist would become an apostle of Jesus and endure the same tortures he had meted out on others. No one knew he would save souls across half the Roman world and some day write half the New Testament for us to read today.

Jesus' Apostles' Persecution & Death

Jesus warned his twelve when he first selected them in

Matthew 10:16-18, 28,

"I am sending you out like sheep among wolves. Therefore be as shrewd as snakes and as innocent as doves. Be on your guard; you will be handed over to the local councils and be flogged in the synagogues. On my account you will be brought before governors and kings as witnesses to them and to the Gentiles. But when they arrest you,....Do not be afraid of those who kill the body but cannot kill the soul. Rather, be afraid of the One who can destroy both soul and body in hell."

The apostle Paul later explained their treatment this way in I Corinthians 4:9-13: " I think, God has exhibited us apostles last of all, as men condemned to Death; because we have become a spectacle to the world, both to angels and to men. We are fools for Christ's sake…we are weak…without honor. To this present hour we are both hungry and thirsty, and are poorly clothed, and are roughly treated, and are homeless; and we toil, working with our own hands; when we are reviled, we bless; when we are persecuted, we endure; when we are slandered, we try to conciliate; we have become as the scum of the world, the dregs of all things, even until now."

Do you think the apostles wondered if all they were going through was worth it?"

Well, the apostle John didn't as much, but the others did. Tradition tells us that...

    Peter was crucified.
    Andrew was crucified.
    James was beheaded.
    John died of natural causes.
    Nathaniel/Bartholomew was flayed alive.
    Philip was crucified
    Thomas was speared through.
    Matthew was speared, then beheaded.

James the Less was sawed in half or stoned.
Jude (Thaddeus) was speared and crucified.
Simon the Zealot was crucified

None of these have been proven, but their Deaths seem to have been caused by jealous pagan priests. Certainly when they closed their eyes in weakness and agony, in the blink of an eye they beheld heaven and glory. They had kept the faith.

The last we see of the apostles is in the last book of the Bible. The twelve foundations of heaven were named after the twelve apostles (Revelation 21:14) and they each had a throne.

"At once I was in the Spirit, and there before me was a throne in heaven with someone sitting on it. 3 And the one who sat there had the appearance of jasper and ruby. A rainbow that shone like an emerald encircled the throne. 4 Surrounding the throne were twenty-four other thrones, and seated on them were twenty-four elders. They were dressed in white and had crowns of gold on their heads" (Revelation 4:2-4) just as Jesus had promised them:

"And Jesus said to them, "Truly I say to you, that you who have followed Me, in the regeneration when the Son of Man will sit on His glorious throne, you also shall sit upon twelve thrones, judging the twelve tribes of Israel" (Matthew 19:28).

Satan Just Thinks He's The Winner

As we have seen, Satan is not omniscient. He does not know all things. He does not know the future. So God gives him his assignment to wreak havoc in this world when all he is actually doing is strengthening his supposed victims. The godly person stands up to the giants and rocks the world.

So, dream on Satan. Your time is coming.

Yes, in the end after Satan has destroyed all the bad leaders, he will be destroyed. He will be the last.

In the meantime, the Christian grows so strong s/he can fight the world single-handedly with smiles and patience and love and never tire of doing so. The "world" hates smiles and patience and love.

King Solomon said thousands of years ago, "If your enemy is hungry, give him food to eat; if he is thirsty, give him water to drink. In doing this, you will heap burning coals on his head, and the Lord will reward you (Proverbs 25:21-22). It was repeated by Paul (Romans 12:20).

What happy weapons God has given us. Every kind of evil will some day be destroyed, "but love never will be conquered" (I Corinthians 13:8). We WILL conquer evil with good (Romans 13:21).

We are more than conquerors through him who loved us. For I am convinced that neither Death nor life, neither angels nor demons, neither the present nor the future, nor any powers, neither height nor depth, nor anything else in all creation, will be able to separate us from the love of God that is in Christ Jesus our Lord. (Romans 8:37-39).

Will it always be easy? No. But we will continue to follow Jesus' example until the fulness of time. Then will come our crown.

18~JESUS' GLORIOUS BODY

The Word of God entered a human body (John 1:1-3, 14). "In the beginning was the Word, and the Word was with God, and the Word was God. He was with God in the beginning. Through him all things were made; without him nothing was made that has been made….The Word became flesh and made his dwelling among us. We have seen his glory, the glory of the one and only Son, who came from the Father, full of grace and truth."

It looked like any other human body. But Jesus' body had special powers the rest of us do not have ~ at least, not yet. An apostle called it his glorious body and says we will have such a glorious body someday. "But our citizenship is in heaven. We eagerly await a Savior from there, the Lord Jesus Christ, who, by the power that enables him to bring everything under his control, will transform our lowly bodies so that they will be like his glorious body" (Philippians 3:20-21).

Although Jesus emptied himself when he came to earth and took on the appearance of a man (Philippians 2:6-8a), he took his glory back after his crucifixion and resurrection (John 17:5).

His Body Had Healing Powers

"And a woman was there who had been subject to bleeding for twelve years, but no one could heal her. She came up behind him and touched the edge of his cloak, and immediately her bleeding stopped. "Who touched me?" Jesus asked. When they all denied it, Peter said, "Master, the people are crowding and pressing against you."

But Jesus said, "Someone touched me; I know that power has gone out from me." (Luke 8:46).

His Body Could Walk On Water

"And the boat was already a considerable distance from land, buffeted by the waves because the wind was against it. Shortly before dawn Jesus went out to them, walking on the lake" (Matthew 14:24-25).

His Body could glow like the sun

Jesus' transfiguration is testified to in Matthew 17:1–8, Mark 9:2–8, and Luke 9:28–36. His body transformed to resemble the sun. (By the way, Moses and Elijah after their death had glorious bodies who could do the same. More on that later.)

His Body Could Become Invisible

" All the people in the synagogue were furious when they heard this. They got up, drove him out of the town, and took him to the brow of the hill on which the town was built, in order to throw him off the cliff. But he walked right through the crowd and went on his way" (Luke 4:28-30).

"Again his Jewish opponents picked up stones to stone him….Again they tried to seize him, but he escaped their grasp" (John 10:31, 39).

"Then their eyes were opened and they recognized him, and he disappeared from their sight" (Luke 24:31).

His Body Could Walk Through Walls

"On the evening of that first day of the week, when the disciples were together, with the doors locked for fear of the Jewish leaders, Jesus came and stood among them and said, 'Peace be with you!' " (John 20:19).

"A week later his disciples were in the house again, and Thomas was with them. Though the doors were locked, Jesus came and stood among them and said, 'Peace be with you!' " (John 20:26).

His Body Could Not Decay

"He spoke of the resurrection of the Messiah, that he was not abandoned to the realm of the dead, nor did his body see decay" (Acts 2:3).

His Body Could Change Shape

In this book's chapter on "Jesus' Life Before He Was Born", it showed how his body could change appearance. It happened again after his death and returning to life:

"At this, she turned around and saw Jesus standing there, but she did not realize that it was Jesus. He asked her, 'Woman, why are you crying? Who is it you are looking for?' **Thinking he was the gardener**, she said, 'Sir, if you have carried him away, tell me where you have put him, and I will get him.'" (John 20:14-16).

"I'm going out to fish," Simon Peter told them, and they said, "We'll go with you." So, they went out and got into the boat, but that night they caught nothing.

Early in the morning, Jesus stood on the shore, but the

disciples **did not realize that it was Jesus.** He called out to them, "Friends, haven't you any fish?" "No," they answered. He said, "Throw your net on the right side of the boat and you will find some." When they did, they were unable to haul the net in because of the large number of fish. Then the disciple whom Jesus loved said to Peter, 'It is the Lord!'" (John 21:3-7).

"**Afterward, Jesus appeared in a different form** to two of them while they were walking in the country" (Mark 16:12). "As they talked and discussed these things with each other, Jesus himself came up and walked along with them; but they were **kept from recognizing him**" (Luke 24:15-16).

His Body Could Soar

"After he said this, he was taken up before their very eyes, and a cloud hid him from their sight. They were looking intently up into the sky as he was going" (Acts 1:9).

His Body Seen Everywhere at Once

When Jesus returns in the clouds, no matter what hemisphere we are in, we will all see him at the same time. People in China and Russia will be able to see him at the same time as people in Europe and at the same time as people in the Americas.

"Behold, He is coming with the clouds, and every eye will see Him" (Revelation 1:7).

His Body is Recognizable to Everyone

When Moses and Elijah appeared at Jesus' transfiguration, no one had to tell Peter, James and John who Moses and Elijah were. When Jesus returns at the end, everyone throughout the world will know who he is.

"Behold, He is coming with the clouds, and every eye will see Him" (Revelation 1:7).

And Our Body Over There?

Is it possible for human bodies to stay young and new and strong? As discussed earlier, Adam and Eve were in the Garden of Eden somewhere around 100 years. After that, they had children. (See Genesis 4:25) And he lived to be 930 years of age (Genesis 5:5).

Adam still had his same body he'd always had. God gave his body strength that he does not give the human body today. If God can do that for the body on earth, the potential is limitless.

God never said he was going to get rid of our bodies and turn us into bodyless spirits. He said our bodies will change. We will have bodies that are perfect and wonderful and imperishable, just like Jesus' glorious body.

"How are the dead raised and with what kind of body do they come? That which you sow does not come to life unless it dies. And that which you sow, you do not sow the body which is to be, but a bare grain, perhaps of wheat or of something else. But God gives us a body just as He wished, and to each of the seeds a body of its own" (I Corinthians 15:35-38).

"The resurrection of the dead is sown a perishable body, it is raised an imperishable body. It is sown in dishonor, it is raised in glory. It is sown in weakness, it is raised in power. It is sown a natural body, it is raised a spiritual body" (I Corinthians 15:42-44).

"Behold, I tell you a mystery; we will not all sleep [die], but we will all be changed in a moment, in the twinkling of an eye at the last trumpet. For the trumpet will sound and the dead will be raised imperishable, and we will be changed. For this perishable must put on the imperishable, and this mortal must put on immortality" (I Corinthians 15:51-53).

"For our citizenship is in heaven from which also we eagerly wait for a Savior, the Lord Jesus Christ who will transform the body of our humble state into conformity with the body of his glory" (Philippians 3:20,21).

Jimmy Allen, Bible professor at Harding University, emphasized Jesus is still a man. He sites I John 3:1-3; I Timothy 2:15, Philippians 3:21, and I Corinthians 15:48-49.

If, in heaven, we will still have some kind of glorified material body, surely God will continue to materialize for us and be on his throne. Since each of us speaks of dying and being with the Lord, perhaps he will be able to be with all multiplied millions of us at once as he does in our prayers today and make us feel as though each one of us is the most important person in the world.

I can hardly wait. How about you?

19 ~ SO WHAT ABOUT HEAVEN?

Ah, home. The road has led us home.

For decades, the author of this book thought heaven was a spirit realm and we would turn into some kind of spirits. But we are going to have glorious bodies in heaven like Jesus' glorious body while he was on earth (Philippians 3:20,21).

Further Colossians 2:9 says "For in Christ all the fullness of the godhead DWELLS in bodily form." Notice, it is present tense. It does not refer to the past only. Therefore, apparently heaven will be material in some way ~ a place where our glorious bodies can and will dwell.

It will be like leaving a dark cave (earth) and entering the glorious sunlight of the ethereal (heaven) which is unspeakable because it cannot be explained.

It is similar to trying to explain color to people born blind. You can say green is like grass and blue is like water, but your words do not come close to describing what color really is. They cannot comprehend color.

It is also similar to trying to explain sound to people born deaf. You can say the high notes are like the hot sun and the low notes like anger. You can say moving up and down the scale to create a song is like leaves dancing in the wind, but your words do not come close to describing what sound really is. They cannot comprehend sound.

So, too, heaven is indescribable because we cannot begin to comprehend it.

But why material? After all, God is a Spirit.

Terrible Things Happen in the Spirit World

When investigating the spirit world, we see that God and his angels are there fighting Satan and his angels. Ephesians 3:10 says the church (individual Christians) display God's wisdom (salvation) to unseen rulers and authorities (principalities and powers) in heavenly places. Ephesians 6:12 says, when we resist or fight evil on earth, we are actually participating in resisting and fighting evil rulers and authorities (principalities and powers) in the unseen world and evil spirits in heavenly places (the spirit world).

More specifically, there are deceiving spirits which are demons (I Timothy 4:1), demonic spirits (Revelation 16:14), impure spirits (Matthew 10:1) evil sprits (Matthew 10:1; Mark 3:11).

There is constant war in the spirit world.

The King of Aram (today's Syria) took his army to fight Israel. When his chariots surrounded the city of Dothan, there was fear everywhere. The prophet Elisha told his servant to look again. When his servant did, he saw the hills and valleys full of angelic chariots of fire. (II Kings 6:13-17).

Daniel 10 says the prophet, Daniel, mourned and prayed for three weeks for God to forgive his sins and the sins of his people, the Israelites. The angel Gabriel appeared to him and said God heard his prayer twenty-one days earlier, but he was so busy fighting the strong prince of Persia (a principality of Satan which Gabriel explained was also the King of Persia) in order to protect God's people, he could not get away. But then the angel, Michael, came to his aid, allowing Gabriel a chance to explain God's answer to Daniel's prayer.

Revelation 9:16 says God's army (his host) is ten thousand times ten thousand. Ten in Jewish number symbolism means all-inclusiveness and multiplying the tens intensifies all-inclusiveness. Therefore, God's army is as innumerable as the stars in the heavens.

Revelation 12:1-9 explains that a woman gave birth and Satan (the dragon) tried to kill her son. He grew up, then there was war in heaven led by Michael and his angels. The war lasted 1260 days which is 3-1/2 years. Remember 3-1/2 years was the length of Jesus' ministry on earth. At the end of those 3-1/2 years, from the cross and the open tomb, Satan and his angels (army) were cast out of heaven. Then in Revelation 12:10-13 the announcement came

> Now have come the salvation and the power
> and the kingdom of our God,
> and the authority of his Messiah.
> For the accuser of our brothers and sisters,
> who accuses them before our God day and night,
> has been hurled down.
> They triumphed over him
> by the blood of the Lamb.

When was the accuser, Satan, hurled down? Not at the beginning of the world. It was at the cross and the open tomb.

Remember in an earlier chapter we discussed that Satan periodically goes to heaven, dares God, does war in some way, and is cast down. (Remember Job 1-3 and the time Jesus' seventy-two were preaching in Luke 10:17-18?)

Jesus said he had command of over twelve legions of angels (Matthew 26:53). At the time of Jesus, a Roman legion of soldiers was fifty-five hundred. So, Jesus was saying he could easily call down sixty-six thousand warring angels to do his bidding.

Daniel 10:20 says Gabriel was constantly fighting the princes of Persia and Greece. In verse 13, Gabriel his referred to fighting the "spirit prince of Persia".

Mark 3:22, Luke 11:15, Matthew 9:34 and 12:24 refer to Satan as being the prince of demons.

Jesus refers to Satan as the prince of this world in John 12:31 and 16:11

The spirit world can be a violent place to be in.

Why War in the Spirit World?

God is Spirit and is everywhere. Throughout the Bible that is stated. There are numerous verses but read them all so this fact can sink in.

1 Kings 8:27 - "But will God indeed dwell on the earth? Behold, heaven and the highest heaven cannot contain You, how much less this house which I have built!
II Chronicles 6:18 - "But will God indeed dwell with mankind on the earth? Behold, heaven and the highest heaven cannot contain You; how much less this house which I have built.
II Chronicles 2:6 - "But who is able to build a house for Him, for the heavens and the highest heavens cannot contain Him? So who am I, that I should build a house for Him, except to burn incense before Him?
Psalm 113:4-6 - The LORD is high above all nations; His glory is above the heavens. Who is like the LORD our God, Who is enthroned on high, Who humbles Himself to behold The things that are in heaven and in the earth?
Psalm 139:7-12 - Where can I go from Your Spirit? Or where can I flee from Your presence? If I ascend to heaven, You are there; If I make my bed in Sheol, behold, You are there. If I take the wings of the dawn, If I dwell in the remotest part of the sea...
Jeremiah 23:23-24 - "Am I a God who is near," declares the LORD, "And not a

God far off? "Can a man hide himself in hiding places So I do not see him?" declares the LORD "Do I not fill the heavens and the earth?" declares the LORD.

Numbers 14:21 - but indeed, as I live, all the earth will be filled with the glory of the LORD.

Deuteronomy 4:39 - "Know therefore today, and take it to your heart, that the LORD, He is God in heaven above and on the earth below; there is no other.

Isaiah 6:3 - And one called out to another and said, "Holy, Holy, Holy, is the LORD of hosts, The whole earth is full of His glory."

Isaiah 66:1 - Thus says the LORD, "Heaven is My throne and the earth is My footstool Where then is a house you could build for Me? And where is a place that I may rest?

Amos 9:2-3 - "Though they dig into Sheol, From there will My hand take them; And though they ascend to heaven, From there will I bring them down. "Though they hide on the summit of Carmel, I will search them out and take them from there; And though they conceal themselves from My sight on the floor of the sea, From there I will command the serpent and it will bite them.

Proverbs 15:3 - The eyes of the LORD are in every place, Watching the evil and the good.

II Chronicles 16:9 - "For the eyes of the LORD move to and fro throughout the earth that He may strongly support those whose heart is completely His. You have acted foolishly in this. Indeed, from now on you will surely have wars."

Zechariah 4:10 - "For who has despised the day of small things? But these seven will be glad when they see the plumb line in the hand of Zerubbabel-- these are the eyes of the LORD which range to and fro throughout the earth."

Acts 17:27-28 - that they would seek God, if perhaps they might grope for Him and find Him, though He is not far from each one of us; for in Him we live and move and exist, as even some of your own poets have said, 'For we also are His children.'

Psalm 34:18 -The LORD is near to the brokenhearted And saves those who are crushed in spirit.

Isaiah 57:15 - For thus says the high and exalted One Who lives forever, whose name is Holy, "I dwell on a high and holy place, And also with the contrite and lowly of spirit In order to revive the spirit of the lowly And to revive the heart of the contrite.

Psalm 145:18 - The LORD is near to all who call upon Him, To all who call upon Him in truth.

Psalm 16:8 - I have set the LORD continually before me; Because He is at my right hand, I will not be shaken.

Isaiah 50:8 - He who vindicates Me is near; Who will contend with Me? Let us stand up to each other; Who has a case against Me? Let him draw near to Me.

Exodus 33:15-16 - Then he said to Him, "If Your presence does not go with us, do not lead us up from here. "For how then can it be known that I have found favor in Your sight, I and Your people? Is it not by Your going with us, so that we, I and Your people, may be distinguished from all the other people who are upon the face of the earth?"

Psalm 14:5 - There they are in great dread, For God is with the righteous generation.

Isaiah 43:2 - "When you pass through the waters, I will be with you; And through the rivers, they will not overflow you When you walk through the fire, you will not be scorched, Nor will the flame burn you.

Zephaniah 3:17 - "The LORD your God is in your midst, A victorious warrior He will exult over you with joy, He will be quiet in His love, He will rejoice over you with shouts of joy.

1 Corinthians 14:25 - the secrets of his heart are disclosed; and so he will fall on his face and worship God, declaring that God is certainly among you.

Joshua 1:9 - "Have I not commanded you? Be strong and courageous! Do not tremble or be dismayed, for the LORD your God is with you wherever you go."

Genesis 28:15 - "Behold, I am with you and will keep you wherever you go, and will bring you back to this land; for I will not leave you until I have done what I have promised you."

Genesis 31:3 - Then the LORD said to Jacob, "Return to the land of your fathers and to your relatives, and I will be with you."

Exodus 29:45 - "I will dwell among the sons of Israel and will be their God.

Leviticus 26:12 - 'I will also walk among you and be your God, and you shall be My people.

Deuteronomy 20:1 - "When you go out to battle against your enemies and see horses and chariots and people more numerous than you, do not be afraid of them; for the LORD your God, who brought you up from the land of Egypt, is with you.

Deuteronomy 31:8 - "The LORD is the one who goes ahead of you; He will be with you He will not fail you or forsake you. Do not fear or be dismayed."

Matthew 28:20 - teaching them to observe all that I commanded you; and lo, I am with you always, even to the end of the age."

1 Corinthians 3:16 - Do you not know that you are a temple of God and that the Spirit of God dwells in you?

John 14:18 - "I will not leave you as orphans; I will come to you.

Ephesians 2:22 - in whom you also are being built together into a dwelling of God in the Spirit.

1 John 3:24 - The one who keeps His commandments abides in Him, and He in him We know by this that He abides in us, by the Spirit whom He has given us.

Psalm 113:3 - From the rising of the sun to its setting The name of the LORD is to be praised.

Psalm 72:19 - And blessed be His glorious name forever; And may the whole earth be filled with His glory Amen, and Amen.

Psalm 96-9 - Ascribe to the LORD, O families of the peoples, Ascribe to the LORD glory and strength. Ascribe to the LORD the glory of His name; Bring an offering and come into His courts. Worship the LORD in holy attire; Tremble before Him, all the earth.

Malachi 1:11 - "For from the rising of the sun even to its setting, My name will be great among the nations, and in every place incense is going to be offered to My name, and a grain offering that is pure; for My name will be great among the nations," says the LORD of hosts.

Revelation 5:13 - And every created thing which is in heaven and on the earth and under the earth and on the sea, and all things in them, I heard saying, "To Him who sits on the throne, and to the Lamb, be blessing and honor and glory and dominion forever and ever."

Satan is jealous. Satan does not want to worship God. Satan wants God to worship him. We see that during Jesus' forty-day temptation when Satan kept trying to get Jesus (God in flesh) to worship him.

Since God refuses to give in to Evil, Satan has tried everything possible to make himself God.

We Are Part of that War

Well, why did God make us part spirit and part material? Why didn't he make us completely spirit? What was just discussed is why. We are too weak to face Satan and his armies in "heavenly places". God's angels are stronger than we are in that respect (Hebrews 1:7), though they are also our ministering spirits (Hebrews 1:14).

Satan has access both to heavenly places and the earth, just as God does. He is prince of this world (John 12:31 and 16:11).

So, God gave us a material body with a spirit and said that this is Satan's domain. Fight Satan where you are. I will not let Satan tempt you more than you can handle (I Corinthians 10:13), but your job is to work against him in his domain.

We are God's warriors against Satan. We are in a battle. Satan fights us with meanness. We fight back with goodness. Satan cannot stand the light and runs from it. Light blinds Satan. Light is more powerful than darkness. "The light shines in the darkness, and the darkness has not overcome it" (John 1:5).

And so, whenever you become sick and refuse to blame and forsake God for it, God wins and you become a hero. Whenever you lose your job and refuse to blame and forsake God for it, God wins and you become a hero. Whenever a tornado, flood, or fire destroy your home and you refuse to blame and forsake God for it, God wins and you become a hero!

What a privilege we have of fighting alongside God, the creator of the cosmos! When you face problems in life and refuse to complain, "Why me?" but stand up and smile, God says, "I am so proud of you!"

There is Only Room Enough in the Spirit World for God

God is everywhere. There are an estimated two trillion galaxies in the universe. That means God is larger than we can imagine.

Not only is there not enough room in the spirit world for Satan, there is not enough room for humans. Remember, God is everywhere including permeating the tiniest atom to the unimaginable gigantic size of the universe.

God never promised us we would be everywhere. Satan is trying it and some day will be destroyed. That is God's domain. But God is love and must have someone to love. So, he created us ~ special us ~ giving us both a material body and part of his spirit. He gave us a material earth to live on.

God Never Promised We Would Be Everywhere

In heaven, God has some sort of material world for us where our "glorious body" ~ which will be just like Jesus' glorious body ~ may dwell for eternity.

If we are going to have glorious bodies like Jesus', our heavenly home will have to accommodate our glorious bodies. I Corinthians 15:35-56 explains that our glorious body will not be ordinary flesh and blood. We have already investigated all the things Jesus could do in his glorious body. We will have those same capabilities, for we will be like him (Philippians 3:21).

Just as it is difficult to explain Jesus' glorious body completely, it is difficult to describe the glorious heaven God has promised us.

What we do know is that, once God's Word took on a human body, Jesus, the Word, will be there eternally with us. He will continue to be the visible image of God (Colossians 1:15) who is actually a spirit and is everywhere.

Ah, so much to comprehend.

Just sit back sometimes and read Revelation ~ the parts that explain heaven to the degree that our finite minds can understand. Although Revelation is completely symbolic, the symbols may also be what they are in order to reveal a glimpse of heaven to us.

Will the streets of gold be moonbeams we can walk along? Will the crystal sea be a sea of stars that will reflect the face of God? I wonder.

God will be With Us in the Heaven He Prepared for us

Yes, Jesus is preparing heaven for us (John 14:3). It will be so "out of this world", we can only begin to imagine what it will be. All we know is that heaven will be glorious in the same way that color would be glorious to a blind person and sound to a deaf person.

Today, our finite minds only glimpse at a small part of what heaven will be. Someday, we will close our eyes here and open them to be welcomed home by Jesus ~ the visible image of God himself.

When Jesus was on earth, we could not see God except by seeing Jesus. Mankind was able to literally see God heal people. Mankind was able to see God suffer, see God become angry, see God weep. Was this a change in God's nature? Check the Psalms. God often suffered, became angry, and wept over us, his children.

In heaven with Jesus still being the image of God in his glorious bodily form, we will be able to see God laugh. Hear God sing. Watch as God opens his arms to us. Yes, in heaven, we will be with God.

Oh, how glorious that will be. Come, Lord Jesus! Oh, that's right. You gave me work to do. Well, as soon as my work is done...

Addendum I

A Few Additional Thoughts
JUST WHO IS SATAN?

Is Satan's Name Lucifer?

Today, it is commonly accepted that Satan's name was LUCIFER who became a fallen angel. Is this fact or tradition?

First, Satan was evil "**from the beginning**" (I John 3:8) and was a murderer "**from the beginning**" (John 8:44). The beginning of what? Compare this to John 1:1-2. "**In the beginning** was the Word. The Word was with God and the Word was God... Through him all things were made; without him nothing was made that has been made." Satan has existed as long as the Word which was God has existed.

Isaiah 14:12-16 (NASB) says, "How you have fallen from heaven, STAR OF THE MORNING, SON OF THE DAWN! You said in your heart, 'I will ascend to heaven; I will raise my throne above the stars of God...I will make myself like the Most High.' Nevertheless, you will be thrust down to Sheol....'Is this the man who made the earth tremble? Who shook kingdoms...'
"

What is the meaning of the word *lucifer?* In the original Hebrew of this passage, the is word *helel and* does not refer to a planet or star. It literally means "shining one" or "light bearer". In the Greek, the word *heōsphoros* means "bringer of dawn", so does not refer to a plant or star either.

In the Latin *Vulgate,* lucifer refers to Jesus and John the

Baptist. It also is used in regard to the Passover candle. Jewish writings have always said the word referred to Nebuchadnezzar, King of Babylon.

Both ancient and modern Jewish scholars have always rejected the idea that Satan was a fallen angel. An association of Isaiah 14:12–18 with a personification of evil, called the devil, developed outside of mainstream Judaism in late so-called Christian writings, particularly with the apocalypses.

In the Catholic apocryphal book of II *Enoch 29:3*, it says, "Here Satanail was hurled from the height together with his angels." This book also says Enoch ascended through ten heavens with the earth being the center. Scholars have traced the origins of the Book of Enoch, not to the Enoch who was ancestor of Noah, but to an anonymous writer at the time of King Solomon.

The Greek Apocalypse of *Esdras 4:32* refers to lucifer as Antichrist. Scholars agree that this book was written around the time the last temple was destroyed around 70 AD.

Two Catholic bishops bore that name:

> Saint Lucifer of Cagliari
> Saint Lucifer of Siena.

Even at the time of the Latin writer Augustine of Hippo (354–430), lucifer had not yet become a common name for the devil.

Martin Luther and John Calvin declared calling lucifer (a description) Satan is from ignorance. THE BEGINNINGS OF CALLING SATAN LUCIFER ORIGINATED IN THE KING JAMES VERSION OF THE BIBLE IN 1611.

Ezekiel 28 pronounces doom on the King of Tyre in

today's Lebanon. Symbolically, this passage could apply only to Adam. Ezekiel 28:12 says he was perfect. When God created Adam, he said in Genesis 1:26, "Let us make mankind in our image, in our likeness." Adam was created perfect.

Ezekiel 28:13 says, "You were in Eden, the garden of God; every precious stone adorned you: carnelian… onyx…gold; on the day you were created they were prepared." Genesis 2:12 mentions the Garden of Eden having onyx, bdellium and gold.

Ezekiel 28:15 says "You were blameless in your ways from the day you were created till wickedness was found in you." Genesis 2:7 says, "And the Lord God formed man of the dust of the ground, and breathed into his nostrils the breath of life; and man became a living soul." We know that everything God created was good.

I Corinthians 15:45 refers to the first Adam and Jesus (the second Adam). Verse 47f says, "The first man was of the dust of the earth; the second man is of heaven. As was the earthly man, so are those who are of the earth; and as is the heavenly man, so also are those who are of heaven. And just as we have borne the image of the earthly man, so shall we bear the image of the heavenly man."

The first Adam was the perfect morning star, the perfect man at the dawn of mankind. The second Adam was the perfect Morning Star as declared in Revelation 22:16.

In Genesis 2:17 God said, "You must not eat from the tree of the knowledge of good and evil, for when you eat from it you will certainly die." When Satan tempted Eve (Adam was nearby to receive his share of the fruit), he said, "God knows that, when you eat from it, your eyes will be opened, and you will be like God, knowing good and evil." Adam did not physically die right then, but his soul did. (Ezekiel 18:20 and Romans 6:23).

Turning the descriptive word of lucifer into a proper noun was a Catholic and Church of England decision.

In Revelation 22:16, Jesus called himself "the root and the descendant of David, the bright morning star". Why would Jesus give himself the same name as Satan? In Revelation 2:28, Jesus said of overcomers he will give them the morning star.

Some say the fall of Satan in Revelation 12:9 came at the beginning. No, it didn't. "The great dragon was hurled down—that ancient serpent called the devil, or Satan, who LEADS the whole world astray. He was hurled to the earth, and his angels with him." Notice, this is in present tense. Satan is always leading the whole world astray.

Revelation 12:10 explains, "…the accuser of our brothers and sisters, who accuses them before our God day and night has been hurled down" further shows this is present tense and is about "our brothers and sisters" who did not exist at the beginning of the world. Satan is always accusing us of our sins.

Revelation 12:11 gives the final explanation: Our brothers and sisters "triumphed over him [Satan] by the blood of the Lamb." Satan was hurled down when Jesus bled and died on the cross.

Satan Falls Periodically

Jesus said after his seventy-two ambassadors returned from their preaching tour, "I was WATCHING Satan fall from heaven like lightning" (Luke 10:17). It was an on-going thing during this gospel campaign. It was not a one-time thing long before.

Thousands of years after the creation, Satan appeared to God and taunted him by saying Job would blame God and forsake him if he had everything taken from him including his health (Job 1 and 2). That jaunt to heaven didn't prove worthwhile to Satan either.

Revelation 12:7-11 says there was war in heaven between Michael and his angels and the dragon (Satan) and his angels. When was he cast out? When the blood of the Lamb was shed and Christians were being persecuted.

> "Now have come the salvation and the power
> and the kingdom of our God,
> and the authority of his Messiah.
> For the accuser of our brothers and sisters,
> who accuses them before our God day and night,
> has been hurled down.
> **They triumphed over him**
> **by the blood of the Lamb**
> and by the word of their testimony;
> they did not love their lives so much
> as to shrink from death."

As we have already seen, Satan has access to God, but doesn't seem to stay long, continually going to heaven and being tossed out.

ADDENDUM II

A Few More of My Thoughts

DOES PARADISE STILL EXIST?

When a Christian dies, people say s/he has gone to be with the Lord. When? The moment they died.

But the same people will turn right around and say there is a "waiting place", half of which is Paradise and half is Gehenna. They'll go into long discussions about the original meetings of those words. They say we stay there until the Day of Judgment. After that, we progress on to heaven.

Let's look at the passage people normally refer to in order to describe paradise, Luke 19:22-26

> 22 Now the poor man died and was carried away by the angels to Abraham's bosom; and the rich man also died and was buried. 23 In Hades he lifted up his eyes, being in torment, and *saw Abraham far away and Lazarus in his bosom. 24 And he cried out and said, 'Father Abraham, have mercy on me, and send Lazarus so that he may dip the tip of his finger in water and cool off my tongue, for I am in agony in this flame.' 25 But Abraham said, 'Child, remember that during your life you received your good things, and likewise Lazarus bad things; but now he is being comforted here, and you are in agony. 26 And [a]besides all this, between us and you there is a great chasm fixed, so that those who wish to come over from here to you will not be able, and *that* none may cross over from there to us.'

What was so special about Abraham? He was the "Father of the Faithful" (Gal. 3:16-29; Rom. 4:11).

"Bosom" was a term used in the first century regarding people who reclined to eat on a low table. The person who was in the bosom of the host had the greatest honor, more so than the person who was immediately at the host's back.

We humans have given this place where Lazarus was the name of paradise, meaning garden. If it was, indeed, paradise was basically where Adam and Eve lived. It was a garden with the Tree of Life in it. God cast them out of the garden, "lest they eat of the Tree of Life and live forever. So, the Tree of Life stayed in the Garden and Adam and Eve left the garden.

The Tree of Life

But, wait! Revelation 2:7 says the Tree of Life is in the Paradise of God. Where is the Paradise of God ~ not the paradise of Adam and Eve but the Paradise of God?

This promise was given to those who overcame in the church in Ephesus. Jesus told the overcomers in the church in Sardis overcomers would wear white garments and walk with Jesus (Revelation 3:4-5). So, where do we wear white garments? Revelation 7:9 says those dressed in white stand before the throne of God.

Further, Revelation 22:1-2 says the Tree of Life is on both sides of the River of Life. And where is the River of Life? Flowing out from the throne of God.

How Did the Tree of Life Get There?

Jesus told one of the thieves on his own cross, "Today, you will be with me in paradise" (Luke 23:43). What happened in paradise? Jesus had a nice visit with Abraham and his children, the children of the Father of the Faithful. Then three days later, he escaped from paradise and returned to earth. So, how did paradise appear in heaven? Ephesians 4:7-10 says this:

> [7] But to each one of us grace was given according to the measure of Christ's gift. [8] Therefore [a]it says, "WHEN HE ASCENDED ON HIGH, HE LED CAPTIVE A HOST OF CAPTIVES, AND HE GAVE GIFTS TO MEN." [9] Now this *expression*, "He ascended," what does it mean except that He also had descended into the lower parts of the earth? [10] He who descended is Himself also He who ascended far above all the heavens, so that He might fill all things.

Who are the captives?

Jesus came to ransom us from Satan. Mankind was still under Satan's power because "the day you sin you will die" (Genesis 2:7). Their souls the moment they sinned and their bodies died later. Remember, Satan is the master of death. "Therefore, since the children share in flesh and blood, He Himself likewise also partook of the same, that through death He might render powerless him who had the power of death, that is, the devil." (Hebrews 2:14).

Jesus paid the ransom he demanded and set us free. "But Scripture has locked up everything under the control of sin, so that what was promised, being given through faith in Jesus Christ, might be given to those who believe" (Galatians 3:22).

So, we see that, when Jesus left paradise, he took all the faithful with him to the Paradise of God. But he could not have done it until he had paid the ransom and come back to life.

What about righteous people who lived before Jesus came? The freedom he brought by paying the ransom was retroactive.

Romans 3:24-26 says Jesus paid the ransom demanded by Satan with his blood so that "God passed over the sins previously committed."

The Hebrew write said it more clearly: "[Jesus'] death has taken place for the ransoming of the transgressions that were committed under the first covenant....He is the mediator of a new covenant so that, since [Jesus'] death has taken place for the ransoming of the transgressions that were committed under the first covenant, those who have been called may receive the promise of the eternal inheritance" (9:15; 10: 15).

When Can The Saved Go On To Heaven?

Remember what people commonly say when a Christian dies? "S/he has gone home to be with the Lord." The apostle Paul expressed the same thing in II Corinthians 5:6-8: "Therefore, being always of good courage, and knowing that while we are at home in the body we are absent from the Lord— 7 for we walk by faith, not by sight— 8 we are of good courage, I say, and prefer rather to be absent from the body and to be at home with the Lord."

He stated the same thing in Philippians 1:23: "But I am hard-pressed from both *directions*, having the desire to depart and be with Christ, for *that* is very much better".

Paul he goes on to say in II Corinthians 5:10, " For we must all appear before the judgment seat of Christ, so that each one may be recompensed for his deeds in the body, according to what he has done, whether good or bad."

Hebrews 9:27 says, "It is appointed unto man once to die and then the judgment." It does not say, "once to die, then paradise, then the judgment."

We see in Revelation the saved being in heaven seemingly before the judgment. Revelation 4:4 says the 24 elders were in heaven, not paradise. Revelation 7:9-10 and 19:1 do not say the multitude was worshipping in paradise; they were worshiping before the throne of God in heaven. Revelation 14:3 says the saved were not standing in paradise; they were tanding before the throne of God. The judgment did not occur until Revelation 21.

So, do we have a contradiction? Not at all. Revelation 10:6 says time will cease. Time does not exist in eternity. Here are some translations of Revelation 10:6 ~

KING JAMES - And swore by him that liveth for ever and ever, who created heaven, and the things that therein are, and the earth, and the things that therein are, and the sea, and the things which are therein, that **there should be time no longer.**

AMERICAN KING JAMES - And swore by him that lives for ever and ever, who created heaven, and the things that therein are, and the earth, and the things that therein are, and the sea, and the things which are therein, that **there should be time no longer.**

DOUAY-RHEIMS - And he swore by him that liveth for ever and ever, who created heaven, and the things which are therein; and the earth, and the things which are in it; and the sea, and the things which are therein: **That time shall be no longer.**

ENGLISH REVISED - And swore by him that liveth for ever and ever, who created the heaven and the things that are therein, and the earth and the things that are therein, and the sea and the things that are therein, that **there shall be time no longer.**

II Peter 3:8 says for God, a thousand years is like a day and a day is like a thousand years.

In eternity, we are no longer in a realm of time (no beginning, no ending and no waiting). In eternity, everything is now, not yesterday or tomorrow. Therefore, when we die and time no longer exists, that moment is the Day of Judgment for us.

When humans travel in time, we travel down a line with a past, present, and future. Imagine an ant traveling on a line drawn on a piece of paper. Now image you looking down on that piece of paper. You are not limited to that line of past, present and future, for you see the entire piece of paper, not just the line. You are not limited to viewing just the line for you can see it all; you are not in a realm of time. In eternity, there is no line ~ no past, present or future; there is no such thing as time.

John Clayton, noted former atheist and director of "Does God Exist?" says this about time (*Wrestling with God's Nature*, Sept-Oct., 2011):

> God is outside of time and space — not three dimensional, not physical, and not human. What is meant by "outside of time" is that God is not limited by time or any time-dependent quantity
>
> In Genesis **1:1** God created space and time. The concept of "beginning" would mean that once space and time were created, gravity wells would have been formed and these would be filled with appropriate masses becoming what Genesis calls "the heaven and the earth."

Nowhere in the Bible does it say we die, then we go to paradise, then we wait for the big day, and then we finally get to heaven. It was the case under the Old Covenant before Jesus died. But they were not waiting for the Day of Judgment, they were waiting for Jesus to ransom them.

But, since Jesus' death and resurrection, everything has changed. We have been set free. We have been ransomed. We have escaped and been given heaven to be with the Lord. Forever. Amen.

Thank You

Thanks for reading my book! I'm so honored that you chose to spend your precious time with my golden thoughts. You are appreciated. I'm an independent author who relies on my readers to help spread the word about stories you enjoy. Would you take a few minutes to let your friends know on Facebook, Pinterest... wherever you hang out online?

Also, each honest review at online retailers means a lot to me and helps other readers know if this is a book they might enjoy,

I welcome contact from readers. At my website (below), you can do so. You can also sign up for my newsletter (below) to be notified of half-price books and new releases.

ABOUT THE AUTHOR

Katheryn Maddox Haddad has a bachelor's degree in English, Bible, and history, from Harding University, a Master's Degree in management and human relations from Abilene Christian University, and part of a Master's Degree in Bible from Harding University, including Greek studies.

She grew up in the cold north and now lives in Arizona where she does not have to shovel sunshine. She basks in 100-degree weather with palm trees, cacti, and a computer with most of the lettering worn off.

She spends half her day writing, and the other half teaching English over the internet worldwide using the Bible as textbook through World English Institute. She has taught some 7000 Muslims, mostly in the Middle East. Students she has converted to Christianity are in hiding in Afghanistan, Iran, Iraq, Yemen, Jordan, Somalia, Sierra Leone, Uzbekistan, Tajikistan, Indonesia, and Palestine. "They are my heroes," she says.

In addition to her seventy-seven books (non-fiction, novels, and storybooks), she has written numerous articles for *Gospel Advocate, Twentieth Century Christian, Firm Foundation, Christian Bible Teacher, Christian Woman,* and several world mission publications. Her weekly column, *Little-Known Facts About the Bible,* appeared several years in newspapers in North Carolina and Texas.

Buy Your Next Book Now

CHRISTIAN LIFE
Applied Christianity: Handbook 500 Good Works
You Can Be a Hero Alone
Worship Changes Since 1st Century + Worship 1sr Century Way
The Best of Alexander Campbell's Millennial Harbinger
Inside the Hearts of Bible Women-Reader+Audio+Leader
The Lord's Supper: 52 Readings with Prayers
http://bit.ly/Christianlife

BIBLE TEXT STUDIES
Revelation: A Love Letter From God
The Holy Spirit: 592 Verses Examined
Was Jesus God? (Why Evil)
365 Life-Changing Scriptures Day by Date
Love Letters of Jesus & His Bride, Ecclesia
Christianity or Islam? The Contrast
The Road to Heaven
http://bit.ly/BibleTexts

FUN BOOKS
Bible Puzzles, Bible Song Book, Bible Numbers
http://bit.ly/BibleFun

TOUCHING GOD SERIES
365 Golden Bible Thoughts: God's Heart to Yours
365 Pearls of Wisdom: God's Soul to Yours
365 Silver-Winged Prayers: Your Spirit to God's
http://bit.ly/TouchingGodSeries

-SURVEY SERIES: EASY BIBLE WORKBOOKS
→Old Testament & New Testament Surveys
→Questions You Have Asked-Part I & II
http://bit.ly/BibleWorkbooks

HISTORICAL RESEARCH BIBLE
for Novel, Screenwriter, Documentary & Thesis Writers
http://bit.ly/32uZkHa

GENEALOGY: How to Climb Your Family Tree Without Falling Out
Volume 1 & 2: Beginner-Intermediate & Colonial-Medieval
http://bit.ly/GenealogyBeginner-Advanced

Connect With The Author

Website: https://inspirationsbykatheryn.com

Facebook: bit.ly/FacebooksKatherynMaddoxHaddad

Linkedin: http://bit.ly/KatherynLinkedin

Twitter: https://twitter.com/KatherynHaddad

Pinterest: https://www.pinterest.com/haddad1940/

Goodreads: https://www.goodreads.com/katherynmaddoxhaddad

Get A Free Book

Sign up for Katheryn's monthly newsletter with half-price books for the whole family and insider tips on what's coming next.
http://bit.ly/katheryn

Join My Dream Team

Members get the first peek at my newest book and have fun offering me advice sometimes. I have a point system of rewards for helping me get the word out. Check it out here:
http://bit.ly/KatherynsDreamTeam